Please return to Dan Hunt
3554 Anderson's Place Lam~
Franklinton NC 27525
919-528-3278

The Tractor in the Haystack

The Tractor in the Haystack

Great Stories of Tractor Archaeology

SCOTT GARVEY

Voyageur Press

First published in 2008 by MBI Publishing Company and Voyageur Press, an imprint of MBI Publishing Company, 400 First Avenue North, Minneapolis, MN 55401 USA

Voyageur Press titles are also available at discounts in bulk quantity for industrial or sales-promotional use. For details write to Special Sales Manager at MBI Publishing Company, 400 First Avenue North, Minneapolis, MN 55401 USA.

To find out more about our books, join us online at www.voyageurpress.com.

Library of Congress Cataloging-in-Publication Data

Garvey, Scott, 1959-
  Tractor in the haystack : great stories of tractor archaeology / Scott Garvey.
       p. cm.
   Includes index.
   ISBN 978-0-7603-3295-5 (hardcover)
   1. Antique and classic tractors--Conservation and restoration. 2. Farm tractors--Collectors and collecting. I. Title.
   TL233.25.G37 2008
   629.225'2--dc22
                               2007049209

Editor: Leah Noel
Designer: Chris Fayers

Printed in China

Contents

FOREWORD

BY ROGER WELSCH

It's an old joke. A man sees a classified ad in the newspaper: "1935 Allis-Chalmers tractor in excellent condition, runs fine, no dents, nothing missing, steel bands over lug wheels, ready to drive away. $75." Of course, he can't believe this offer could possibly be true, but he calls the number anyway, and the woman says no, he's reading the ad right. So he follows her directions to check it out, and sure enough, there is that gorgeous tractor in mint condition. And no, the price isn't a mistake—$75 and it's his. Astonished, he hands her the cash and loads the tractor, but then can't resist asking her why she would ever sell this beautiful machine at such a bargain price.

She explains: "A couple of weeks ago my husband ran off with our babysitter and just wrote me from the Bahamas saying I should sell his stuff for whatever I can get for it and send him a check. And that's exactly what I'm doing. Would you perhaps also be interested in a Winchester Model 21 presentation twelve-gauge shotgun in mint condition for, oh, $25?"

My academic training is as a folklorist, and I have often been asked where jokes come from. As often as not, they start in truth—or maybe more precisely, truths. I don't know where this joke started because I had heard it before I ventured out to a farmstead twenty years ago or so to look at a nice little antique tractor that was listed with a price that seemed hard to believe. And yet there it was, just as advertised. And yes, that was the price the lady wanted. Hmmm . . . the lady. . . . Soooo, the tractor belonged to her husband? And he wasn't there because . . .

You guessed it. The tractor was indeed the fallout from a nasty divorce, and all she wanted was (1) to get rid of it and (2) get a price that would not just put some money in her pocket, but would gall the living bejeepers out of her ex-husband.

You can imagine my dilemma. I'm a man. Should I participate in such an evil plot, or should I, in solidarity with men everywhere, tell this woman what I thought of her pernicious scheming? I looked at the tractor, I looked at the tight-jawed, thin-lipped woman. I looked at the cash in my hand. And I decided that there was probably nothing more in this world her former husband would want than for another good tractor lover to pick up his old tractor at whatever price, the cheaper the better, and show it the love he would have given it had he not done something really stupid like leaving the toilet seat up for the millionth time and thereby lost all his rights to peace, home, and tractor. Conscience clear, I loaded up the tractor and brought it home.

This book tells us stories like that. In this world, you can tell at least twenty stories about tractor deals gone sour for every one about a stunning bargain. But to me, tractor restoration seems to be a game of good feelings, and bum deals just don't have much of a place in the hobby's tales of found treasure. Instead, we old-iron enthusiasts like to regale each other with stories of amazing finds, unlikely surprises, unbelievable bargains, gifts, goodwill, fun, and good fortune. For us, these are the modern legends and fairytales of our lives.

Or maybe, there actually are more good stories than bad ones. Heaven knows, I've had my share of both. However, as I consider the last twenty years, the good tractor stories are the ones I remember best.

A friend gave me my first Allis WC, and even though it had been sitting in a woodlot gathering mouse nests, bird poop, sticks, and leaves for two years, a cup of gas and a bit of a pull started the sweet little Allis right up. We drove her up the ramps onto my friend's trailer, and from that very moment I was captivated by the adventure and romance of old tractors.

The magic didn't stop. Maybe the third or fourth Allis WC I picked up came to me through a scrawled letter from a farmer not far from where I live. He had heard I liked old Allises, and he wondered if I might be interested in his old WC. I went to look at it, and it was sitting in shed right where he had parked it thirty years earlier, dry and relatively clean . . . considering. This one didn't start right up, but it rolled easily up onto the trailer. As we left with this bargain I got for little more than its value as scrap iron, the seller came out of his house waving some papers at us. Uh-oh . . . what's the problem? No problem. He just wondered if I'd like the operator's manual, parts book, and receipt he got when he bought that machine originally in 1937. The papers were in even better condition than the tractor.

I got a WC wreck once in exchange for some of my books. As I dismantled it for parts, I found that only four bolts were holding the oil pan on the block. Hmmm . . . someone must have been working on this machine when it was parked decades before. I dropped the pan and took a peek. Wow. Whoever had worked on that machine had put new pistons and bearings in it before giving up—easily worth more than I had paid for the whole machine.

And there was the time two friends and I drove the good part of a day to get to a Kansas scrapyard where I had bought two Allis WCs sight unseen. Or, as it turned out, what used to be Allis WCs. Now they were nothing but wrecks with everything of value already robbed off the carcasses. All that fuel, all that travel, all that work for nothing but a load of junk. But as we were ready to pull out of the yard, frustrated and disgusted, the scrap dealer said casually, "Did you want the wheels that go with those tractors?" Wheels? Uh, what wheels? "Those over there leaning on that tree."

And there were two pair of back wheels with lugs, one a rare set of "spider" or skeleton lugs, the other an equally interesting double-size lugged set. "And over there . . . all I have is the one pair." He was pointing at a set of front steel wheels in excellent condition. We could have dumped the tractors and just taken home the wheels and come out ahead of the deal. Just like in the fairytales.

I've gotten my tractors as gifts, in exchange for books, on a dare and a bet that I'd never get that wreckage running again. And I've been stung with deals that were indeed way too good to be believed.

There are a lot of books about the nuts and bolts of tractor restoration. I've written a few of those myself, but what this book deals with to me, as an anthropologist, is an equally interesting aspect of the hobby (or maybe the word should be obsession)—the *human* element. Those of us who love old iron try to justify ourselves with practical rationale: We restore old tractors as a matter of recycling, we say, of solving small problems, enjoying of small, sometimes even large, victories, and having control in a world that sometimes seems so out of control.

In our private moments, however, when we are in the company of other collectors and restorers and when we feel safe about being completely honest, we tell the real stories about why we do what we do: surprise, mystery, hope, good fortune, and sometimes, yes, outright magic. This book is about that. Read on about the adventures and good fortune of others, and dream about your own chances of lost treasures rediscovered. Somewhere out there, an ancient tractor is sitting in a woodlot, sagging barn, or old haystack, just waiting for *you*. Let the stories in this book serve as your appetizer, while you wait for the main course.

Roger Welsch is a longtime tractor enthusiast and the author of numerous books of fiction, folklore, and humor, including Forty Acres and a Fool: How to Live in the Country and Still Keep Your Sanity; Love, Sex and Tractors; *and* Everything I Learned about Women I Learned from My Tractor. *A cross between Erma Bombeck and Dr. Ruth— except he's male and lives in Nebraska—Welsch is best known for his appearances on the CBS Sunday Morning show, where he offered up observations on rural and small-town life on the plains.*

ACKNOWLEDGMENTS

Well, where do you start to thank people for sharing their stories in a book like this? There have been so many who have graciously shared their personal adventures with me that it really is impossible to name them all. In many cases, I was just a voice on the phone or someone at the other end of an email message. The fact that most collectors didn't just hang up on me is, in itself, a wonder.

But talking to, emailing, and meeting so many people in the world of old-tractor collecting has revealed at least one thing to me: There are some extremely nice men and women involved in this hobby. And the old tractors— be them McCormick, Huber, Silver King, or any other—are the glue that holds this "family" together.

Among the members of the family who I would like to single out for mention are the following: J. R. Dailey, whose assistance was invaluable in kick-starting my research; Brian Holst at the John Deere Collectors' Center for his assistance; and David Hogan for freely offering the benefit of his IH experience.

And, of course, I am grateful to everyone whose personal story appears in the book. All of you have been very generous in sharing your experiences and pointing me toward others who share the same passion for their restored tractors. I thank you all.

Unfortunately, not all the stories I found could be included in the limited space available in this book. That doesn't mean those personal experiences were any less deserving, and editing the final manuscript was far from easy. So, I'm grateful to all of you whose stories don't appear here, as well.

Whenever you work on a project where you meet people who you are better off for knowing, you know the experience was worthwhile. And because of that, I know I'm a little better off for having been involved with this book.

INTRODUCTION

Every tractor enthusiast with a pulse has a tractor or two stuck in his (or her) memory that he wishes he hadn't sold; or if it belonged to Dad, Grandpa, or someone else, he wishes he could find it again. For many of us, those special tractors are an integral part of some fond memories of days gone by—of simpler, happy times when there was great satisfaction in completing a hard day's work.

A couple of years ago at an auction sale, I saw just how strong the ties between a farmer and his tractor really can be. Every year, I wait with bated breath for the spring auction sale season to start. I always peruse the sale listings, looking for interesting tractors that have been dragged out of the tall grass behind a farmyard to clean out the place for the new owner. Sadly, too many of the current sale posters offer only late-model, 200-plus-horsepower machines that will sell for thousands less than their owners paid for them new, thanks to depreciation.

However, a few gems show up each year that demand my attendance at these sales, even if I just get to look at the tractor and watch someone else buy it. I make sure I don't get carried away and bring home too many old tractors— the idea of sharing sleeping space in the doghouse with Rover keeps that practice firmly in my mind.

At one particular sale near my home in Saskatchewan, Canada, in 2004, a nice example of a John Deere Model 3020 was up for sale. Despite going out of production by the end of 1972, these tractors are not rare old machines by any stretch. Model 3020s made their way down Deere assembly lines for nine years and were widely distributed across the North American prairies—not to mention many other regions—in the tens of thousands. Yet this particular tractor, as it turned out, was certainly one of those machines that someone wished he hadn't sold.

When the auctioneer finished selling off all the small items and implements, he finally got around to offering the tractors. Of course, as is usual, the crowd grew more attentive now that the big-ticket items were being bid on. The first of three tractors to sell was a nice—if uninspiring—example of a 3130 John Deere. Then the auctioneer climbed up onto the platform of the 3020 for a commanding view of the crowd.

Bidding on the 3020 started off normally. Yet as the sale continued, one older gentleman and his wife, who were standing very close to the tractor, raised their bid almost immediately each time the auctioneer looked at them. Soon, everyone realized that, for some reason, this retired couple wanted that tractor badly.

Slowly, word passed through the crowd of onlookers that the elderly bidder and his wife had owned this tractor once before, and they traded it in to the local dealer for a newer model many years ago. Now the couple had long-since retired and no longer had any real need for a tractor. Still, the couple really wanted it and after offering a bid of $7,400, the auctioneer dropped the hammer, pointed at them, and said, "Sold!"

Instead of quickly moving on to sell the remaining tractor, the auctioneer paused for minute. He announced to the crowd that Bud and his wife—the buyers—had purchased that tractor new in 1964 from the local John Deere dealer and, as fate would have it, the owner of that dealership just happened to be in attendance too. The dealership owner, who was also now retired, then reached up and took the ignition keys from the auctioneer and, in front of the crowd, presented them to Bud and his wife for the second time. Applause erupted, along with a round of congratulations.

The spontaneous celebratory mood seemed perfectly natural to all who were in attendance. Yet would someone without such close ties to farming understand the significance of reuniting with a thirty-plus-year-old tractor? That's hard to say. One thing seems certain though. Just like the loyal farm dog, many of the reliable tractors that spent so many hours sharing hard work with us on the farm seem to have become family members. As if they were favorite sons, many farmers take pride in the shiny green, red, yellow, or any of a myriad of other-colored machines that once graced their homesteads. Coming together again with an old mechanical coworker after years spent apart, it seems, is as heartwarming as any family reunion.

When asked what he was going to do with the tractor, Bud didn't seem to really know. He just wanted it back. If you're not the least bit surprised by this, then you understand the sentiment that has fueled the tractor collector hobby over the past few decades. You may even share in it.

Old tractors are now not just denizens of the open countryside; they're sometimes found sharing a space in urban garages with the family minivan. And why not? Old tractors are more than just symbols of the progress of mechanized technology. They are a link with the past. Perhaps more accurately, they are a link with an ideal— the thoughts and memories of sitting in the doorway of a barn's hayloft on a summer evening, with your legs dangling out high above the ground, watching cows come and go. And of course, your ever-present farm dog is beside you, looking over the vast golden fields.

You didn't need flashy, violent video games back then to amuse you. You had a whole world that was waiting to be explored, and a lot of it was seen from a hay wagon behind a tractor and baler. It's no surprise, then, why old tractors figure so prominently in your memories.

For those who didn't have the opportunity to grow up on a farm—and there are more and more with each passing decade—you have really missed something priceless. Maybe the world would be a little better place if every city home had an old tractor in the driveway, and someone could explain to the next generation that this trusty machine is really a symbol of the best values in life: honesty, responsibility, and a willingness to contribute, among others.

Oh, if only, there was a world where everyone had an old tractor.

CHAPTER ONE

Finding Favorites

The Case in the Shed

As far as J. R. Dailey of Lexington, Kentucky, is concerned, there's only one brand of tractor: Case. His passion for Case tractors, it turns out, has also been passed down to his children and grandchildren, just as if it was part of the family's distinctive DNA. Maybe taking part in the family's annual Case tractor run that J. R. organizes is what makes so many of the Dailey family members want to have their own restored Case tractor.

To satisfy the family's demand for classic Case tractors, at least ten of them have passed through the Daileys' workshops. The Cases often go in as derelict hulks and come out resplendent in shiny, new coats of Flambeau Red.

After leaving farming in 1972, J. R. began operating a service station, and his sons frequently helped out in the service bays. Now that he's retired, his mechanical skills, and those of his sons, find an outlet in tractor restorations.

But you can't restore tractors if you can't find them. That's no problem for J. R., though. His reputation as a dyed-in-the-wool Case enthusiast has helped him track down some of his favorite machines. Aside from his activities in organizing Case events, J. R. has his own website, and that brought at least one special tractor his way.

In 2001, Kenny Hillman of Cynthiana, Kentucky, took notice of J. R.'s website and decided to send him an email. A 1954 Case VAC-14 had been sitting inside a shed on Kenny's farm long enough, and Kenny wanted to get rid of it.

After chatting on the phone with Kenny, J. R.'s interest was piqued, and he decided to make the fifty-mile journey from Lexington to Cynthiana to see the tractor. When J. R. arrived, Kenny directed him down a trail that led deep into the heart of the farm property. After driving along the trail for some time, the two men came upon a once-proud farmstead that had previously belonged to Kenny's neighbor; it was now well hidden amid a stand of trees. The old house had fallen down, but a log barn was still standing. Still, cows hadn't been kept in there for years. Nearby was the tractor J. R. had come to see.

The VAC-14 was now the only support for the shed it had been parked inside of many years ago. The shed roof had fallen down on the tractor, and all that could be seen was the tractor's grille poking out from under a mass of weathered old boards.

Kenny Hillman's neighbor parked this Case VAC-14 in a shed and removed its front axle after being injured when another VAC-14 rolled over on him. The tractor outlasted the shed. This is the sight that greeted J. R. Dailey on his first visit to the Hillman farm.

J. R.'s grandson, Kevin, stands in front of the tractor after all the old shed boards were removed and the tractor was fully revealed. It took a full day to clear the debris and load the tractor onto the trailer for the trip home.

Kenny purchased the farm behind his original holdings several years ago, and the tractor, along with everything else in the old farmstead, had been left behind. Kenny had known the old farmer well; he passed away not too long after Kenny bought the farm.

Having lived so close by for so long, Kenny also knew the history behind the VAC-14. The former owner had parked the tractor in the shed after an accident that nearly killed

> By the time Kenny decided to sell the Case, time had taken its toll on it, as it had on the buildings. Still, J. R. saw a potential addition to the family fleet.

him. The old farmer had originally owned two VAC-14s. When using the other tractor around the farm, it rolled over and seriously injured him. Determined to ensure no one else would ever suffer such a fate, Kenny's former neighbor parked the second VAC-14 in the little shed and removed the front axle from it, leaving it on blocks. That way the tractor could not be driven and could never hurt anyone. And there the tractor had stayed ever since. A look through the old barn turned up the Case's missing front axle and a few other parts.

By the time Kenny decided to sell the Case, time had taken its toll on it, as it had on the buildings. Still, J. R. saw a potential addition to the family fleet. With a 124-cubic-inch engine that only produced 22 horsepower, the little tractor wasn't a powerhouse, but it would fit in nicely with the rest of the entrants in the family's forty-mile tractor rally. Its size would also make it a useful machine for a variety of chores around J. R.'s home.

A few days later, at nine o'clock in the morning, J. R., his son Allen, and his grandson Kevin returned with a four-wheel-drive pickup truck and trailer to load the old Case. They needed the four-wheel-drive truck to get into the old yard site and make sure they could haul the tractor out without trouble.

Kevin Dailey takes the wheel of the now-restored VAC-14, two years after his grandfather paid Kenny Hillman $400 for the tractor that was hidden under a collapsed shed.

When Kevin saw the tractor, he immediately told his father and grandfather that he wanted to purchase it for himself. So Dad and Grandpa allowed fifteen-year-old Kevin to pay Kenny the $400 and become the tractor's official new owner. Kenny agreed to throw in a plough, cultivator, and a few other implements that were lying around. First, though, they had to get the old Case out of the shed.

The only way to move the tractor was to disassemble the shed board by board. By the time the Case and its implements were loaded on the trailer, it was four o'clock in the afternoon. Soon a tired trio headed home with the newest addition to their tractor family.

Once inside Allen's workshop, the group pored over the VAC-14 and carefully took stock of its condition. Not everything was rosy with the old Case. At some point in time, coolant had frozen inside the engine and the block had cracked as a result. That meant a replacement needed to be found before the tractor would run again. Luckily, J. R.'s collection of tractors and spare parts made that an easy chore. The tractor also needed its rear rims replaced; its tires had gone flat years before and the rims sank into the ground and rusted. Other than that, the tractor was okay.

Still it took Allen and Kevin about two years to get the tractor in working order. It was then up to J. R. to put a new coat of paint over the fully restored tractor to give it that final touch. Now, what once was a rusty, partly disassembled hulk could easily pass for a tractor that had just rolled off the assembly line—providing, of course, you were willing to believe it was 1954 all over again.

My First Ford

By Chris Britton,
Belleview, Florida

I had a New Holland tractor for my regular farm chores, but I had always wanted an older tractor to work on, specifically an old Ford. At that point in time, I didn't know the difference between a 9N or an 8N, and I was completely unaware of the 2N.

Years later, when I saw an old Ford on the side of the road while traveling from my day job to my night job in July 2002, I was immediately interested. I was already running late, so I couldn't stop longer than a minute to jot down the phone number and give the tractor a quick once over. Still, I decided I wanted it—no, needed it!

When I got to work that evening, I called the fellow who owned the Ford. We negotiated a price and set up a time for me to come out and look at the tractor again in the morning. I assured him that if the tractor ran I would buy it. An hour later the gentleman called me back and said he had just sold it. Well, how was that for luck? I had the tractor itch, and now I had no way to scratch it.

25

Over the next few weeks, I searched high and low for
Ford tractors. Most of the ones I saw were so beat up they
were nearly unrecognizable, or they were so expensive
that I didn't even bother to go look at them—well, actually
I did go look at them. I just didn't tell the wife.

Finally, while shopping for farm supplies at a Tractor
Supply Company store near my farm, my luck changed.
While in the store, I had to make a trip to the restroom.
On the wall by the restroom doors were advertisement
boards where people could pin up ads and business cards. I
happened to spy a 3×5-inch, somewhat grainy picture of a
Ford tractor. The ad said the tractor ran great and had lots
of new parts. The tractor also was decent looking, and the
owner only lived about fifteen miles down the road from
me.

I drove up with the wife the next day to see it, and
we started kicking the tires. I took my trailer with me,
remembering that the last time I stopped to look at a
tractor it was sold out from under me. I also thought about
a strange pattern that had been occurring lately. My wife
and I would see an item for sale sitting on the side of the
road for six months with no bites. Then, we would stop and
look at it, and while we were there, someone else would
show up and buy it. So we decided—before this trip out
to see the 8N, I'd like to point out—that if we thought we
wanted something, we would take the means to buy it and
bring it home right then and there.

In addition to that, I think showing up with a trailer
gives you a bit more bargaining power; the seller knows

you can take it if the right number comes up. So now I always load up my checkbook and trailer and head out.

As usual, the photo hid the Ford's small imperfections, which became blatantly obvious when I inspected the iron in person. I was almost sold on it when I noticed that the wiring was a nightmare. I listened to the fellow try to explain how it was set up, how it was positive ground, and how to use jumper cables to do this or that, and so on. Clearly, I could tell the electricals were going to need some help. I think the fellow must have sensed what I was thinking because he turned back around and said, "Yeah, it may need some wiring. I'll knock off a hundred bucks for you to get some wires." That pretty much sold it.

After making the deal, the Ford crawled up onto the trailer under its own power—a definite plus! After hitting the road, the very next thing I did was stop at the farm supply store on the way home—with the tractor in tow—and buy an I&T FO-4 service manual. Given what I saw of the wiring, I knew I was going to need it.

I figured my first task was to locate the 8N's serial number and then make a list of all the parts I would need to start fixing up the cantankerous old girl. I already had decided it was cantankerous because while unloading it from the trailer, the Ford ran out of gas—or rather I forgot to turn the gas on. A minor detail—the tractor's fault, not mine.

After finding the serial number and making a list of the obvious parts I would need, I called one of the popular online parts houses. Luckily, the fellow on the other end of the phone knew what he was doing because I sure didn't.

All this tractor lingo hadn't set in with me yet: side mount versus front mount distributors, doglegs, radiator pads made of hair, and all the rest.

When all was said and done, I ordered a set of headlights, a wiring harness, all the tie-rod ends and drag-link grease cups, an air breather tube and connectors, clamps, an oil filter, an ignition coil, and a handful of lug nuts and studs. I also decided to replace the winged catch on the battery box door. The previous owner, a cabinet maker, had used big decorative cabinet hinges and wood screws to repair the battery door cover. The cabinet-style latch was . . . uh . . . nice.

Within the first few days of working on the Ford, I learned just how challenged my new tractor's electrical system was. My fiddling had made it a nonstarter. I really didn't have a lot of mechanical experience at the time. I could change oil or headlights, and as a teenager I did the front brakes on my car. That was about the extent of it.

Despite the previous owner's claim that the generator had just been rebuilt, it was no longer working. So I sent it off to a local rebuilder, and I also installed a new regulator and ammeter. I also discovered one other little problem that was the likely source of all the electrical trouble. The tractor had a six-volt electrical system with an eight-volt battery. After getting the generator back and installing everything, I was very relieved when the tractor started and charged correctly. Now on to the next task.

My next phase of repair was actually initiated by my wife, who noticed that the end of one of the three-point hitch's lift arms had been welded. She thought I should

Found languishing on acreage near his home, Chris Britton's Ford 8N had serious electrical problems. Connected to a battery with too much voltage for its six-volt system, the tractor's wiring was nearly burned out. The Ford also needed a long list of other parts replaced.

replace it so it would "look better." I assured her the arm had probably functioned that way for many years, but she kept mentioning it every day. So I finally gave in and went to the farm store again and picked up a new lower lift arm. That was the coolest thing, I thought, being able to run into town and get readily available parts for a fifty-year-old tractor.

I had figured this for an easy job: Slip the old one off and put the new one on. But wait, unlike my newer tractor whose lift arms are held on by lynch pins, these were held on by nuts—old nuts . . . old, rusted nuts . . . old, badly rusted nuts!

This job turned out to be a learning experience, the kind that required a trip to the discount tool store. I had never used a nut splitter or a torch before, but I learned quickly. There was no other way to get those fifty-year-old, badly rusted nuts off so I could replace the lift arm. The engineer who designed that particular piece must have chuckled heartily to himself as he thought of other people trying to change it. In fairness, though, the procedure went well. I only started one small fire in the process.

In the midst of all this mechanical activity, I was running some errands for my job a couple of cities north of where I live, and I passed by a tractor dealer. I noticed he had a Ford NAA on the lot. I stopped to look at it, and the salesman came out. The thing was crusty, rusty, and really beat up, but it ran. He threw me the keys and let me play with it. When I asked how much, he threw out a number that made my trigger hand twitch. I paid with my credit card, zoomed back to work, took an hour off, went home, picked up the trailer, and managed to get back to the dealer just as he was closing. Thankfully, the tractor was still there waiting for me.

When I got it home, I threw a tarp over it. I wasn't sure how I was going to explain to my wife that I bought another tractor while the first one wasn't even finished. On the weekend, she noticed the NAA hiding under the tarp and commented, "Oh, I see you bought a parts tractor for the other one." I mumbled something like, "Uh, yeah, right." Later, when she caught me working on it, I tried to sound convincing by telling her it was in better condition than I thought, so I couldn't bear to part it out. She's a pretty smart lady, though. She didn't fall for that.

Since buying these tractors, I have ended up with all sorts of tools I never knew I would ever use or need, including a big, beefy pipe wrench, which was responsible for removing about half of the stuck nuts on the 8N. And by December, after sacrificing many nights and weekends—along with suffering skinned knuckles and pinched fingers—the 8N project was completed. And I had finally been able to scratch my tractor itch. I now had a fine example of an 8N in my yard, not to mention the rusty NAA.

Shortly after finishing the job, I went out one chilly morning to use the newly restored tractor and found the starter firmly locked up. So it was back to the FO-4 manual and online discussion forums to figure that one out. Did I say the 8N project was completed? Uh, yeah, right.

A Transcontinental
Team Effort

If you're an old-tractor collector, the larger your network of friends is, the better your chances of finding that one special machine you just have to have in your stable. For John Boyens of Bettendorf, Iowa, a chance meeting with a native of the Netherlands turned out to be the key in finding a rare Farmall FC-D to add to his International Harvester collection, as well as added one more person to his circle of good friends.

John Hammink of Anna Paulowna in the Netherlands, a fellow IH enthusiast, first met John Boyens at the Red Power meet in Bloomfield, Missouri, in 1994. John Hammink's attraction to American IH models brought him to the states in search of replacement parts for the North American machines in his collection. After meeting Boyens, Hammink often hit his new friend up for leads on parts to keep his Dutch friends' tractors running.

The two kept in touch regularly over the span of several years, exchanging everything from email to Christmas cards. On occasional U.S. visits, Hammink made a special trip to see Boyens so they could talk about their shared passion for red tractors. During one of Hammink's visits, he and Boyens met up in Atkinson, Illinois, for another one of those chats that often seemed to center on their International Harvester machines.

"I commented that Farmall had at one time made a Super C diesel in France and asked him if he'd ever seen one," Boyens said. Later, Boyens mentioned that he would like to have one of those rare Farmalls in his collection, if he could ever find one. John Hammink apparently didn't forget that conversation because his Christmas card in 2004 included a short note that mentioned finding an FC-D on a dealer's lot in Belgium.

Finding the tractor came after Hammink did some detective work on behalf of his American friend. During his visit to the Red Power Euro convention in Germany that year, Hammink managed to find someone who knew the whereabouts of a little FC-D, and he was directed to a Belgian tractor dealer. Hammink eventually made the trip to Belgium, took a picture of the little tractor, and emailed it to Boyens.

Although the tractor was a little worse for wear, Boyens immediately knew he wanted to add it to his collection. It was apparently working on a Dutch farm until it was traded into the dealership, and it was still in good working order. It did look a little tired, though. The little tractor probably had seen its fair share of road miles, as the tires had excessive tread wear.

Today, after its long journey across the ocean, the FC-D is at home amid the other pieces in John Boyens' IH collection. Every time Boyens sees it, he remembers his Dutch friend with the same first name, who hunted down the tractor as a favor.

Boyens' Dutch friend helped him secure the sale of the tractor, but getting it shipped across the Atlantic would take some organizing. Fortunately, Boyens had another friend with exactly the right connections to help get that job done. Neil West, another collector who lives near Boyens in Iowa, has a passion for old Lanz tractors and equipment, which were built in Germany before that company was taken over by John Deere. In order for West to get most of the Lanz pieces in his collection, he had to buy them in Europe and arrange to have them loaded into shipping containers for the trip back to the states. Fortunately, West was in the process of loading another container that was going to be shipped from the Netherlands and there was room in it for the FC-D.

Arjan Van Lenthe, West's man on the ground in Holland, picked up Boyens' newly acquired FC-D and loaded it into the shipping container. The transportation arrangements seemed to be going smoothly until Arjan realized he needed a special type of wood blocking to be placed in the container, securing the tractor for shipping. He had to travel to Germany to get the wood, which was treated with pesticide so that the container would enter the United States without risk of importing any unwanted wood-borne insects or diseases. The chemical used to treat the wood was banned in Holland.

Today, after its long journey across the ocean, the FC-D is at home amid the other pieces in John Boyens' IH collection. Every time Boyens sees it, he remembers his Dutch friend with the same first name, who hunted down the tractor as a favor. Sadly, John Hammink died unexpectedly just before the FC-D started off on its ocean voyage. He may be gone, but John Boyens certainly won't forget him.

Forgotten, but Not Gone

When Gene Connelly parked his 1939 Allis-Chalmers Model B along the fence shared with his neighbor's property nearly twenty years ago, he probably didn't think it would stay there so long he'd forget about it. That's what happened, though. When Gene and his neighbor Wayne Assay were mowing brush along the shared fence line years later, they rediscovered the old tractor. By then, it was completely hidden by the brush and trees that had grown up around it.

When unearthed, the little B still had the homemade dozer blade attached to it that had kept Gene's driveway cleared of snow during the Ohio winters. Gene grew hay on his small farm near Mogadore, Ohio, for years, and at some point the B had been an integral part of his operation. But in 2003, when the tractor emerged from under the brush it had been hiding in, he had long-since retired.

Although Gene only exhibited a brief "oh, yeah" moment at the sight of the B, Wayne almost immediately thought of his nephew, Steve Assay. Steve (who is formerly from that area of Ohio) and his family have a passion for old tractors—even though they live in Lakeland, Florida. Suspecting Steve might be interested in the B, Wayne gave him a call. Steve was interested and quickly reached an agreement to buy the old tractor. Soon enough, he was on the road with his truck and trailer, making the 1,100-mile trip back north to Ohio.

By the time Steve reached Ohio, the damp fall weather had set in, turning the Ohio clay into a sticky gumbo that made extracting the B from its decades-old hiding spot even harder. The B wasn't in the best of spots to begin with, so thankfully, Steve's one-ton Chevy had four-wheel drive. Even that wasn't enough. Before the B could be moved, Steve, Wayne, and Gene needed to do some more clearing. One tree had grown up right through a gap in the tractor, and it took a few minutes with a chainsaw to cut it down before the B was clear of its entanglements. Then Steve's fears proved true. When trying to load the tractor, the truck got hopelessly stuck. It couldn't move itself, let alone pull the weight of the trailer and the B, which was chained behind it.

Fortunately, Steve had an old friend who still lived in the area, and he owned a four-wheel-drive truck, too. After a quick phone call, Steve's friend showed up to help. With his friend's truck chained to Steve's, which was hooked to the trailer, which was chained to the B, the train of vehicles slowly moved forward out of the mud and onto drier land.

After completing its cross-country trek, the B was put into Steve's shop so he could begin removing parts and discovering exactly what restoring the tractor held in store for him. With help from his stepfather, who was a heavy-duty diesel mechanic, Steve tore down the tractor. The sheet metal was in remarkably good condition, considering the tractor had been exposed to the elements for decades. The engine was another story. Steve estimated he took three gallons of water out of the crankcase, which went a long way toward explaining why it took more than a little effort to free the stuck parts inside the block.

Once that was done, Steve realized the engine was salvageable. After the block came back from a local machine shop and it was reassembled with the necessary replacement parts, the engine ran smoothly.

The little B now makes the rounds to various shows in the Florida area. Although Steve loves to compete in vintage tractor pull competitions with other tractors in his family's stable, the B isn't included in that activity. "I don't like to work it too hard," he said.

So, now that it no longer has to bale hay or clear any Ohio snow, and is excused from tractor-pulling events, it leads a more leisurely life in its retirement—feeling right at home in Florida.

Finding a Namesake

If you're an eight-year-old boy with an interest in farm tractors and you suddenly find out there is a brand of tractor with your name on it, you probably immediately start dreaming about parking one in your own garage. For Marvin Huber of Quincy, Illinois, that dream eventually came true.

He first found out about Huber tractors in fourth or fifth grade, when he had to do a research project. "I could pick any subject I was interested in, so I decided to write about tractors. I researched it and found out about Huber tractors." From then on, the appeal of finding and buying one of his namesake machines never left him.

Marvin was raised on an Illinois farm, and although agriculture was in his blood, he decided working on farm machinery was preferable to working in farm fields. So eventually, he became the service manager at a John Deere dealer in his hometown.

That connection with John Deere led to Marvin meeting one of the foremost Huber tractor collectors in the United States, Don Huber—no relation to Marvin or the tractor company. Don had worked for John Decre, too, and at one point he called the Deere dealership Marvin worked at in Quincy looking for a little help in shipping a Huber tractor to his home in Moline. Don had bought a Huber near Quincy, and the staff at the dealership helped load and ship the old tractor.

Some years later, when a Huber tractor showed up on the listing of an antiques auction near Mount Alburn, Illinois, in 1993, Marvin called Don to see if he was interested in it. When Don decided not to attend the sale, Marvin thought he would go and see if he could get the tractor for himself.

The 1927 Huber 20-40 was still a one-owner tractor. Although it still ran, it was really showing its age; it was definitely a mechanic's special. Fortunately, Marvin was a mechanic. The color of the tractor was a little unusual, too.

The tractor's original owner was still alive, but he was elderly and unable to attend the sale. Marvin did, however, learn a little bit of the tractor's history from the owner's grandson, who was there and knew the tractor well. The original owner, Marvin was told, had bought the tractor new in January 1927 and faithfully parked it inside a shed every night. The owner had even laid planks on the shed's dirt floor to keep the steel wheels off the ground to prevent excessive rusting. All that care had kept this tractor in running order for decades.

About ten years before that auction, the owner decided the tractor needed a new coat of paint, so he looked around and found a color that matched what was on the tractor. By then, though, the tractor looked gray because the original

The elderly original owner of this Huber 20-40 faithfully kept it hidden inside a shed for the entire life of the tractor. He even put planks on the ground to keep the tractor's steel wheels off the dirt floor to prevent rusting. Only when the owner's property was to be auctioned off did the tractor's existence become widely known.

olive drab green that the Huber Company had used on its tractors had faded. Because Huber was also building military machines at the time, the manufacturer simply painted its farm tractors with the same army paint in name of efficiency. Unfortunately, the owner chose more of a light gray paint for the respray. As a result, the new paint color was far from historically accurate. It seems the man had owned the tractor for so long he forgot what color it was when he first bought it.

A check of the serial number showed that the Huber was the 45th tractor built out of only about 365 similar models. It had a lower hood line due to its smaller, 35-gallon gas tank. When a larger, 55-gallon tank was included on later models, the hood had to be raised in order to squeeze it in. That really changed the entire look of the tractor.

This Huber also had the Super Four 536-cubic-inch engine. It was a giant displacement for the tractor's humble horsepower output, at least by today's standards. To help reduce the high inertia forces on the large pistons, the Super Four engine was equipped with aluminum connecting rods—a feature that's more at home on a NASCAR track today than tractors of the 1920s. Of course, the tractor was built during the age of experimentation in tractor design.

Determined to try and outbid all other contenders for the Huber, Marvin and his father-in-law, Don, patiently waited as the auctioneer sold a seemingly endless supply of antiques. Eventually, the auctioneer announced that the Huber and the other tractors would sell at one o'clock. As the sale progressed, Marvin noticed one man stand out among the crowd. He had been one of the most active buyers, purchasing many of the antiques. After the auctioneer's announcement about the sale time for the tractors, this man began carrying off his purchases and carting them to his nearby home.

Marvin turned his attention back to the auctioneer as time for the tractor sale approached. The Huber was first up on the block. Bidding on the tractor was brisk, with several people interested in it. Before the sale, Marvin thought he would be able to take home the Huber for about $3,500, but the bidding had already surpassed that mark before Marvin could even get into the fray. Eventually, Marvin's bid of $5,250 won the day.

A few minutes after the hammer fell on the Huber sale, the fellow who had earlier been furiously buying antiques came running up insisting he wanted to buy the tractor.

The man hadn't realized one o'clock had passed, and by the time he returned from taking home his earlier purchases, he had missed the Huber sale. He was irate about it. "He definitely got a little nasty," Marvin said. Yet his venting couldn't change the fact that the Huber was now Marvin's, and Marvin wasn't about to give it up.

Once the tractor was safely home, Marvin looked it over, and even though the old tractor was running, it was in dire need of an overhaul. Marvin's friendship with Don Huber proved to be indispensable in getting the old tractor restored. Marvin was able to get a few hard-to-find pieces from Don's personal stock of Huber parts. Rebuilding the engine still required some ingenuity. Most parts just weren't available anymore.

Once again, the help of friends was invaluable. Another Huber enthusiast and restorer shared a tip: The piston rings on the Huber were of the same diameter as the rings on one of Ford's engines. The Ford's rings were only half the thickness, though, so Marvin had to put two Ford rings on in the place of one original. The engine now runs smoothly, with excellent compression.

Marvin says he doubts the size of his Huber tractor collection will ever rival that of Don Huber's, but having this tractor in his garage has allowed him to finally fulfill the dream that started when he was a boy in elementary school and first saw some tractor pictures in a book. Yes, dreams really do come true. Sometimes, it just takes a while.

The Inspired Apprentice

Offering them free to a good home may be a way owners part with puppies and kittens, but not old tractors—even ones in rough shape. However, that's the deal Lyndon Van Eck struck with his uncle for the ownership of a 1948 John Deere Model D.

Only sixteen at the time, Lyndon was spending the summer working on his uncle's farm near Claresholm in Alberta, Canada. He already had a fascination with old machinery, and his uncle's farmyard was the perfect place to poke around and search for hidden mechanical treasures, which seemed to be almost everywhere.

The one thing that held his attention was what was left of the old D, which was sitting near one of his uncle's machinery sheds. "I asked my uncle about it, and he said that my grandfather—on my mother's side—had bought that tractor from a local farmer to use for parts," Lyndon said.

A lot of the D's pieces were scattered around the farm. The grille and radiator assembly were under a stack of old lumber, the starter and seat were hidden in a corner of an unused workshop, one front wheel hub was in an old storage shed, and the magneto was under a workbench in a Quonset hut.

Lyndon had been itching to try his hand at a restoration and thought working on the D would be a perfect first project. All he had to do was convince his uncle he was capable of tackling such a job. "My uncle was a little skeptical about whether I could get the D running or not. He saw no value in it. He said that I could have it if I could load it and haul it off his yard." To that offer, Lyndon had only one thing to say: "Deal!"

When the summer was over and Lyndon's father was due to come and pick him up, Lyndon phoned home and asked his father if he would bring a trailer with him. He explained the deal he had made with his uncle, and his father agreed to rent a flat-deck trailer to haul the old tractor home.

Getting the D on the trailer wasn't easy. It had to be lifted on. "I used my uncle's 4020, which had a monster of a loader on it," Lyndon said. "On the first try, we didn't have the chains hooked to the 4020 in the right places, so when we lifted, we almost tipped the 4020." The second effort was successful, and the old Deere came off the ground.

After getting the tractor home, Lyndon began thinking he had bitten off a little more than he could chew with the old D. "I found out it had quite a bit of internal damage," he said. So he decided to set the project aside for a while. He would leave it until he had a little more experience under his belt. He also thought about keeping the D as a parts donor, a job it had been relegated to many years prior by his grandfather.

Still curious about the tractor's history, Lyndon had a conversation about it with his grandfather, who told him

Lyndon Van Eck found this 1948 John Deere Model D sitting neglected and partially dismantled in his uncle's farmyard. The tractor had a connection to both of his grandfathers. One had owned it, and the other had operated it when the tractor was in its prime.

the name of the person he bought it from. When Lyndon happened to mention that name to his father, it sparked a thought. His father remembered that Lyndon's other grandfather—on his father's side—had once worked for the previous owner as a farm laborer. The odds were good that Lyndon's other grandfather had spent a lot of time in the seat of the old D when it was in its prime. Suddenly, the tractor had a double family connection, and leaving it as a parts donor just didn't seem right.

"My parents thought it was kind of neat that I was getting into old tractors. They figured that such a major project would keep me out of trouble for quite some time," Lyndon said.

Eventually, the D will run again, once Lyndon has the experience needed to tackle some major reconstruction work. He is now an agricultural mechanic's apprentice working for a machinery dealer in the nearby town of Barrhead. In the meantime, he keeps his eye out for other potential restoration projects, which led him to another interesting find.

Lyndon's coworker, Marvin Peters, was sent out on a service call to a farmyard about eight miles from town. Two hours later, the fellow tractor enthusiast showed up back at the shop grinning as he related an interesting piece of news. "He asked me, 'Do you know anything about Massey 55s?'" Lyndon said.

While Marvin was working on a machine in one farmer's yard, he noticed a tractor sitting just on the opposite side of a fence in another farmyard. It was an old Massey-Harris 55. It looked like it had been there quite a while because one tire was flat and the grass had grown up all around it. It certainly hadn't seen any recent use.

However, this Massey looked different than others Marvin had seen before. It had an arched front axle. It also had very large, original-looking rear tires. As Marvin described the tractor to him, Lyndon realized the tractor wasn't a plain old 55. Neither one of them could think of a reason for the difference in design, and it certainly warranted further investigation.

Conveniently enough, Marvin had to go back to get some information off the tractor he had originally gone out to fix, so Lyndon went along on the trip back to the farmyard. After finishing off the job they were sent out to do, they strayed across the fence to make a closer inspection of the 55.

It was clear the 55 was some kind of Western Special, but the model number stamped on the serial-number plate raised a few more questions. It read 55D1WH. The only way to solve the mystery was to hit the reference books, but Lyndon could only find mention of a 55D1SH Diesel Western or a 55G1WH Rice Special. Neither one fit the bill.

"Finally, I asked a couple of my buddies, who were big Massey gurus," Lyndon said. "It turns out that between them they had two Westerns with that model number." The tractor was a wide-axle version of the Western. That design gave the tractor a little more width and height, which gave it an imposing appearance.

"Well, my interest was definitely piqued," Lyndon said. "I went to talk to the owner of the 55, but found that the tractor had been moved into a shed." Apparently, the tractor was suddenly attracting too much attention for the owner's liking. According to its owner, the Massey was a 1953 model and had been in the family since it was new. Then came the classic line: He was going to restore it when he had a little more time.

"Oh, well," Lyndon thought. "Plenty more tractors are sitting in back corners of yards or sheds just waiting to be found!" And in the meantime, that leaves all the more time to devote to the D.

An A for an H

In the 1960s, Don Beingessner was really into cars. "I collected a lot of old parts cars and parts for cars," he said, and he used many of those parts to restore a variety of old classics. When the appeal of spending weekends and evenings under the hood of a car diminished, Don found himself spending less and less time with his old hobby. He still kept a few parts cars on hand, though, as well as others waiting for restoration.

Among them was a 1928 Model A Ford that had been converted into a pickup truck. Trucks like that are relatively rare, and Don knew it was too good to abandon. He didn't have any immediate plans to make it operable again, so he decided to just hang onto it, saving it for a rainy day.

Eventually, Don found himself in need of a small tractor to handle odd jobs around his yard, so he bought an 8N Ford. It needed a restoration, though—a task that Don really enjoyed. Soon, tinkering with tractors became more important than his previous car hobby.

As it turned out, the 8N was a perfect first effort. "I always liked smaller tractors," Don said. And the little Ford fit that description nicely.

As he thought about it, he realized that the tractor's owner probably had a strong interest in old cars, considering the collection on the property. That gave Don an idea. . . . Maybe this could be the rainy day for which he was saving the Model A truck.

In the mid-1980s, Don was on a duck-hunting trip and happened to drive through the small town of Simpson, Saskatchewan. Among the few buildings within the village's limits were those scattered on a couple of old farmyards, one of which attracted Don's attention. This yard had a house, a barn, and a couple of run-down, old buildings. It also had a bunch of old cars scattered about in the grass.

Still harboring an appreciation for some of the classics, Don scanned the yard as he drove by, just to check out what old cars might be hiding there. One machine caught his eye, but it wasn't a car. It was a little John Deere Model H tractor. It was the only tractor, in fact, among the forest of old cars.

"I always liked John Deere tractors," Don thought, so he stopped for a closer look. He decided he would like to have it, particularly because it fit in well with the small-tractor theme that inspired him.

As he thought about it, he realized that the tractor's owner probably had a strong interest in old cars, considering

This John Deere Model H caught Don Beingessner's eye as it sat beside an old farm building, along with a group of old cars. The owner was more interested in cars than tractors, so Don offered to trade his 1928 Model A Ford truck as an even swap for the H.

the collection on the property. That gave Don an idea. Maybe the guy would be interested in another old automobile—a rare one. Maybe this could be the rainy day for which he was saving the Model A truck.

So with a plan in mind, he pulled into the yard and knocked on the door of the house. A man about thirty years old answered. Don introduced himself and asked about the H. "First I asked if the tractor would be for sale, and he didn't commit himself," Don said. "Then I mentioned the Model A truck, and he seemed quite interested in it." So far so good, at least he didn't get a flat no yet.

After spending a few minutes looking at the John Deere, Don and the owner of the H struck a deal. Don would take the H, and in return, he would deliver the Model A Ford truck to the old farmyard. It would be a straight swap.

"He didn't even come and look at [the truck]," Don said about the tractor's owner. "I just described it to him and he was happy with it."

About a week later, Don loaded up the Model A truck and headed out to Simpson to complete the deal. After arriving at the old farmyard, the man took a look at the truck on Don's trailer and confirmed he was satisfied with it. So Don unloaded it and pulled the H onto the trailer. There was also a little bonus to go along with the tractor. The owner had a box of new John Deere parts to throw in with the deal.

After getting the H home and unloaded, Don did what you would expect: He put it into the workshop for a thorough inspection. The sheet metal was in pretty good shape. The paint was faded, though. It also needed a couple of minor touch ups—nothing major. "I didn't have any trouble getting it going," Don said. After draining the stale fuel, cleaning the carburetor, and adding fresh engine oil—and a few of the other usual efforts required in coaxing an engine back to life after a long period of sitting idle—the tractor fired and ran smoothly.

The H has yet to undergo a complete restoration, but when it does, Don already has the box of spare parts that came with it to cut the cost down. "I don't even remember what's in it," Don said. "I just packed it away." So far, the H has been running reliably whenever Don decides to fire it up, so extra parts haven't been a concern.

With a meager 12-horsepower output at the PTO, the H is no powerhouse. Even modern lawn tractors boast higher numbers than that. Don is still happy with it, though. It was just one of those tractors a collector with a passion for smaller models just had to have.

Meeting His Waterloo

Barry Bromley was bitten by the entrepreneurial bug early in life. At the age of eighteen, he went to a farm auction and bought a McCormick W-4 tractor for $500. In 1958, he hitched it to his father's John Deere 14T baler and went around the Manitoba countryside custom baling for other farmers, pocketing eight cents a bale for his efforts.

One fall day, Barry found himself at a farm about seven miles from his home, baling straw for the Robins family. While he was waiting in the field for an empty hay rack to arrive, he was having a casual chat with Neville Stevenson, a relative of the Robins family who he was helping with the harvest. The conversation eventually turned to John Deeres, and Neville commented that Barry should go and see the old Waterloo Boy tractor that had spent years parked behind the barn in the Robins' farmyard.

"I was aware of the Waterloo Boy and that John Deere had bought the company in 1918, but I'd never seen [a Waterloo Boy tractor] or any detailed pictures," Barry said. But on that day in 1958, he got a firsthand look at one.

When Barry asked Reg Robins, one of the brothers running the farm, about the tractor, he found out his father

Barry Bromley and his friends commemorated the first working day for the Waterloo Boy tractor by posing for photographs. Until Barry found it, the 1923 Model N had been nothing more than a roosting place for turkeys behind a barn in a neighboring farmyard.

bought it new. Since Reg's father had passed away, no one on the farm had any interest in it. It hadn't been used in years. Reg then asked Barry if he wanted to buy it.

The tractor was a 1923 Model N—and, of course, it was the great-grandfather of the modern John Deere line of tractors. It was parked in some tall grass and covered with a lot of turkey manure when Barry and Reg walked up to give it a once-over. It had certainly seen better days.

"It had sunk close to a foot into the ground," Barry said. The fuel line was missing and some bolts had come out of the angle grouser lugs on the wheels, but it wasn't seized.

The old tractor was rare, even in 1958. Despite that, few people could see anything but a lot of scrap steel when they looked at it—except Barry. "People generally disregarded them," Barry said of the prevailing attitude toward outdated tractors in the 1950s and 1960s.

The tractor was almost complete, except its radiator had been taken off and was never replaced.

Taken with the old, steel-wheeled machine, Barry couldn't get the tractor out of his mind. So after thinking about it for almost a week, he made a deal with Reg. He paid only $35 for the rare tractor. With its purchase, Barry's personal fleet of tractors was now two—the Waterloo Boy and the W-4.

When Barry went home and broke the news to his father about his latest purchase, he didn't get much in the way of support for making a shrewd business deal. "My father never really appreciated my interest in machinery," Barry said. "He wondered why I wasn't interested in guns."

The following Sunday morning Barry and his younger brother returned to the Robins farm to pick up the Waterloo Boy. Reg Robins helped out by getting the steering loosened up after finding it was stuck because the tractor had been idle for so long. The group replaced the missing grouser bolts and, after greasing the wheels, they chained it behind the W-4 and tugged the old tractor out of its longtime parking spot.

Before they left with the tractor, however, Reg had something to show Barry. He handed Barry a letter he had just received from someone in Saskatchewan who wrote to say he would pay $100 for the Waterloo Boy. Reg was a man of his word, so he honored the agreement with Barry, even though he could have sold the old tractor for triple the price Barry paid.

After a slow trip down the road, the two tractors pulled into the Bromley family's farmyard at around noon on what turned out to be a warm and pleasant October day. Once the Waterloo Boy was safely home, Barry and his brother cleaned it up and tried to get it running again.

The missing radiator prevented the boys from starting the old tractor until they could find a replacement. Getting an original part would be nearly impossible. Their only hope was to find a suitable stand-in that would fit. Fortunately, Barry's father was a member of a local grain-elevator association and knew of an old stationary engine that had been removed from one of the association's facilities. The discarded engine had a radiator with it, and Barry's father thought it might work as a replacement. "He told me I could have it," Barry said. The new radiator was much bigger than the original one, but it easily fit into place.

That winter, Barry put the Waterloo Boy into a small workshop on the farm and set to work trying to get the tractor up and running again. When he went to clean out the engine crankcase, he found some ice in it, so he thoroughly flushed it to remove all contaminants. The next step was replacing the old fuel tank, which had completely rusted out. An unused ten-gallon drum was pressed into service as a replacement. Reg Robins had thrown in a new magneto and a new lining for the clutch, which had been bought as replacements but never installed. Once those parts were in and a mouse's nest was flushed out of the replacement radiator, the tractor fired to life.

Barry never had any serious intentions of making the old tractor work for its keep. Yet once it was running, he wanted to have a little fun with it. The following summer, on a Sunday afternoon in July, Barry decided to give the old tractor a chance to stretch its legs. Some of Barry's friends stopped by the farm for a visit, and it seemed like the perfect opportunity to show off the old Waterloo Boy.

Barry, his brother, and friends hitched the tractor to a plow and put it to work on a small plot of land near the farmyard. Seeing the old Waterloo Boy back plowing fields again was a bit of a novelty, and Barry and his friends had to take a picture of themselves with the old tractor to commemorate the event.

Later on, Barry started up the tractor now and again for a chance to drive it around or perform some minor farm job. At some point, a wrist pin set screw came out, and despite replacing it, the screw kept working loose. Eventually, the persistent problem sidelined the tractor. "I got busy with farming and just parked it," Barry said. Once again, the Waterloo Boy sat idle.

In 1971, Barry moved to his own farm, and a few years later he hauled the Waterloo Boy to his new place. The tractor remained parked outside, waiting for another chance to shine. Eventually, that opportunity came.

In 1993, another tractor enthusiast noticed the rare machine in Barry's yard. He tried to convince Barry to part with it, but Barry wasn't about to do that. Instead, they worked out a deal that would see the Waterloo Boy get a full restoration, and Barry wouldn't have to lift a finger. In return, the tractor fan would get a lease on the tractor that entitled him to have possession of the Waterloo Boy for a specified period.

Just to see what it could do, Barry hitched the Waterloo Boy to an old plow and went to work on the edge of a field. It easily handled the job, but a problem with a wrist pin in the engine sidelined the tractor for years—until it was "found" in Barry's farmyard by a restorer.

Once the agreement was made, the tractor was completely overhauled and restored. After the lease period expired a few years ago, the good-as-new Waterloo Boy came home to Barry's farm. The tractor now makes the rounds to local tractor shows and is one of the few examples of its kind left. That rarity makes the old Waterloo Boy a pretty valuable commodity, and it's a classic that is sought after by collectors worldwide. These days, its approximate value is measured in the tens of thousands.

Not a bad return on a $35 investment.

Buckthorn–Brush Moline

Justin Kutka has some fond memories of his former neighbor, Lynn Warriner. Back in 1995, when Justin was just a teenager and lived with his family on a rural acreage near Eagle, Wisconsin, Mr. Warriner lived on the farm next to them. He had been living there for a long time. "He was usually a very friendly guy, but he had a fiery temper," Justin said. "Sometimes little things would set him off, like talking about quack grass. He'd go on and on about it."

When Mr. Warriner reached his mid-sixties, he decided he'd had enough of agriculture and wanted to sell the farm, quack grass and all. Yet over the course of his lifetime, he had accumulated a lot of old equipment that hadn't been used in years. It was now strewn about the farmyard, creating an unappealing sight for potential buyers.

One day when Justin was talking to the old farmer, Mr. Warriner had a proposition for his young neighbor. "You know, Justin, I could really use some help to get my yard cleaned up to sell the place," he said. In return for his help, Justin could have the 1940 Minneapolis-Moline RTU that had been sitting in an overgrown corner of the Warriner farmyard for years.

Almost invisible—except in winter when the leaves fell off the bushes that had grown up around it—this Minneapolis-Moline RTU was part of Justin Kutka's reward for working at his neighbor's farm for a summer.

In need of a parts tractor to aid in the RTU's restoration, Justin found this RTN in the back lot of a local hardware store. After buying it, he found the serial number was only about 1,000 away from the RTU's.

That was an opportunity that really appealed to Justin. Even though he was still only a high school student, he had already restored a 1940 John Deere Model H; he really wanted to find another tractor to work on.

"You could kind of see it in winter when the leaves were off the buckthorn," Justin said. But getting the RTU moved from its longtime hiding spot would be no easy task. The mass of buckthorn bushes that had grown up all around the tractor was a real obstacle. "It was a mess to get at," Justin said. But after a lot of cutting and chopping, the RTU emerged, and Justin and his father managed to tow it back to their yard.

As the yard-clearing project progressed over the summer, Mr. Warriner began giving Justin more implements from the yard. Eventually, Justin had to borrow a friend's tractor and front-end loader to move them all home. The list of old machinery Justin earned included two ploughs, a corn picker, and a bale elevator, to name only a few.

As an added bonus, Mr. Warriner threw in another old tractor that had been hiding in the farmyard: a Massey-Harris 101 Junior. The little Massey was in rough shape. Restoring it would require a major effort. It would more likely end up as a parts donor.

As Justin started moving the implements home, Mrs. Warriner had her own request. She wanted him to get rid of an old New Holland baler that had been sitting in the farmyard for years, in plain sight. She was ready for the eyesore to disappear.

When he had completed the yard-cleaning project, Justin found himself with a pretty large collection of miscellaneous equipment, and shortly after the work was done, the Warriners sold the farm. The elderly couple then headed for retirement in Texas, leaving Wisconsin, Justin, and the RTU behind them.

Once Justin dismantled the RTU with some help from his father, who was a millwright, the real mechanical condition of the tractor became apparent. The four-cylinder engine, which had two separate blocks, had a piston stuck in one of the cylinders. Justin and his father tried all the tricks they knew to free it. Finally, they turned to a hydraulic press to force out the piston, but all that force simply broke the wrist pin free while the piston head remained firmly stuck. However, that effort managed to expose another problem: There was a crack in the cylinder wall of the block about one-eighth inch wide. The block, therefore, was useless.

Still, neither Justin nor his father was willing to give up on the RTU just yet. The tractor had a great deal of potential and was mostly complete. If they could just find a replacement block, work could continue. If they couldn't find a block by itself, then a parts tractor might be the answer.

A few days later as Justin drove down a highway near his home, he caught a glimpse of an old Moline in the backyard of a hardware store. He had noticed the tractor even before Mr. Warriner gave him the RTU, but on this occasion he finally realized it looked like the same model as his RTU. And since he needed a parts tractor, it might be worth it to stop in and see if the Moline was for sale.

After a change of plan, Justin decided to restore the RTN and used the RTU as a parts donor. The two old Molines were eventually merged into one beautifully restored tractor.

The store where the old tractor was sitting sold an eclectic mix of items, from ordinary hardware to ten-foot-high fiberglass animal sculptures. "It had a little of everything," Justin said—including the tractor the storekeeper agreed to sell. It turned out to be a 1940 RTN. It had a single front wheel, rather than the two wheels the RTU was equipped with. More important, the basic tractor design was the same. "I was able to buy it for what I considered to be a very reasonable price," Justin added.

Once the RTN was home, Justin and his father re-evaluated both the tractors. The RTN was a rarer model, so Justin and his dad decided to make the RTU the parts donor. When they checked the serial numbers of the two tractors, amazingly, they were only about 1,300 apart.

In 1999, three years after the restoration project began, the RTN rolled out of the workshop; in the end, it was a joint effort between father and son. After the restoration was complete, Justin sent Mr. Warriner some pictures of the end result of merging the RTU and the RTN. "He was moved to tears. . . . He was mighty happy that his tractor had gone to a good home," Justin said.

A short time later, Mr. Warriner passed away. The RTN, made up of the best parts of two tractors, is now a special machine that Justin expects to keep around for quite some time. "I have something that I'll always remember him by," he said.

CHAPTER TWO

Junkyard Deals

Deere Hunting

N eil West might have had the best job any vintage-tractor collector could wish for. As an engineer working in John Deere's grain harvesting division, he traveled around the United States—and the world—participating in field trials of Deere combines. When he found himself in the heart of one of many different farming communities with free time on his hands, he was able to do a little hunting—Deere hunting, that is. Over the years, his conversations with the locals and the drives he took around the countryside helped him find an impressive seventy-eight tractors for his collection.

Sitting up high in a cab-over truck borrowed from a local John Deere dealer, Neil West was able to spot this Model D, which was almost hidden by brush alongside a road near Kaplan, Louisiana.

One of the most productive expeditions for Neil was a trip to Louisiana's Cajun country during the 1980s. He was overseeing a rice-harvesting combine trial. When he wasn't busy with the new combines, he was scouring the rural countryside for vintage tractors. By borrowing a truck from a local Deere dealer, he had a higher vantage point to see over the tall grasses and trees along the ditches that offered hiding places for old iron.

One Sunday afternoon, Neil remembers following a local farmer down a dirt road that led well off the beaten path; they were in search of an old tractor. Neil had been asking around if anyone could point out a possible addition to his collection—preferably something old and forgotten. That resulted in him following this farmer to a spot that was well-hidden in the trees, invisible from any road.

With the humid conditions, getting to the mystery machine required a little sweat. When they finally made it to the right place, the farmer said, "I think there's a tractor in there." Looking closer, Neil found a styled John Deere Model D that had been rolled over by a bulldozer that was clearing trees some time ago. Neil immediately bought it, despite its sorry state. He knew the tractor would never be a runner, so he stripped all the useable parts off the tractor and hauled them out of the bush. Looking back on it, Neil doesn't want to tackle a job like that—fighting with rusted bolts in those hot, muggy conditions—again any time soon.

The parts scavenged from the old D were eventually loaded onto a pallet for shipping. Fortunately, there was room on a company truck taking combine parts back to Moline, and Neil's parts were able to squeeze in and hitch a ride back home to the Quad Cities area of Iowa, where Neil was living.

As the days went by, Neil found more and more farmers wanting to talk to him. "They found out there was a Yankee around who would pay good money for a tractor they thought was junk," Neil said. From then on, he didn't have any problems finding farmers willing to show him old tractors hiding in every conceivable spot in the Cajun back country. By the time he had finished with the combine project, he had basically drawn a Louisiana treasure map of old tractors. So once the combine project ended, he and a friend returned with a pickup truck and trailer to dig out those treasures and get them home. After they had made their way back to Louisiana, the total number of Deeres they were able to pull out of the undergrowth grew to thirteen.

Getting some of those tractors free from their longtime resting places required a little muscle. So, once again, the local John Deere dealer—who had probably sold many of those old tractors as new machines—came to the rescue and loaned Neil and his friend a large truck with a winch to help in the effort. After the tractors were pulled out, the back lot of the dealership was used as a staging area to get them ready for the long trip back to Iowa. On one occasion, when Neil was working late with his friend to get the tractors ready for the trip, their activities caught the attention of a local policeman patrolling the area. "He checked on us to see what we were up to," Neil said. "Once we told him what we were doing, everything was okay."

As productive as the Cajun adventure was, perhaps his most memorable find was his John Deere 1937 Model AOS. This tractor is a basic Model A, modified with streamlined sheet metal for orchard use—hence the inclusion of OS in the model designation (Orchard and Streamlined). He found it, again, thanks to a tip from a local resident in Logan, Utah, where he was working during a long-term harvesting trial in 1999. He was told there was an unusual-looking old Deere sitting along the side of the road in a junkyard near the town of Willard.

When he drove over to get a look, the sight that greeted him seemed a little like something from a movie. He saw the junkyard owner sitting on a ragged old sofa on the front porch of the run-down house, which also served as an office. Judging by all appearances, it seemed the owner managed to find time to drink a few beers while sitting in exactly the same spot. After getting permission to go

This Model D was in the same field, also hidden by brush. The owner had to mow down the growth around it before Neil could get near enough to work on loading and hauling it away.

through and take a closer look at the tractor that was sitting in the weeds along the edge of the yard, Neil realized it was a relatively rare AOS model.

The yard contained mainly old cars and trucks, and the AOS was one of the few tractors. Although it was clear that this wrecking yard was still in business, it wasn't exactly a hive of activity. The man on the sofa seemed a little surprised that Neil would have any interest at all in the old tractor. He insisted that he would need to get $75 for the scrap value of the steel in it. Neil gladly paid the money, rented a trailer, and hauled it away.

With only a little more than 800 AOS models ever produced, the old tractor was certainly worthy of a $75 rescue and an attempt at a restoration effort. Neil managed

The elderly man standing beside this John Deere Model D also owned the other two tractors in the previous photographs, but he had forgotten about them until Neil spotted them from the road.

to get it into the workshop at the host farm where the combines were being tested, and the farmer allowed him to use the facilities there to start working on the AOS. Neil first discovered the engine was stuck, so he took the head off. The farm workshop happened to be equipped with a high-temperature hot-water system used for some plastics construction, which allowed Neil to run two hundred–degree hot water through the block, alternating the flow with cooler water until the expansion and contraction of the metal made it possible to turn the flywheel with a bar and free the stuck pistons. Incredibly, after freeing the pistons and reattaching the head, the engine fired and ran.

After spending its working life in one of the orchards east of Salt Lake City and almost coming to a sad end in a wrecking yard, the AOS is now restored and one of Neil's prized Deeres.

After a career working to improve the engineering designs built into John Deere's line of machinery, Neil now spends much of his time restoring the designs his predecessors at Deere developed. That makes him wonder about whether someday in the future someone will be hunting Deeres with Neil's designs and spending time working to bring them back to life.

Despite having to work through hot and humid conditions, Neil and a friend were able to recover and load a total of thirteen tractors and some spare parts to send back to his home in Iowa.

Back from the Brink

Don Richards and his family have been in the business of selling International Harvester machinery since 1929, so they're no strangers to red tractors. Today, their dealership is located in Stouffville, a town just north of Toronto, Ontario. Being near the industrial heart of the country, they were close to International Harvester's manufacturing and distribution center in Hamilton, Ontario, for years. Machinery bound for dealers all across Canada came from IH's dock warehouse facility at the Hamilton plant.

"We found that, in the mid-1950s, the most practical way for us to get new equipment was to pick it up at the Hamilton plant," Don said. So for years, he and other members of his family made frequent visits to the dock warehouse.

"Sometime around 1966 or 1967, there were two British-built IH B614 tractors that turned up at the plant, and they were used to tow wagonloads of components from one area of the plant to another," Don said.

For years these tractors were part of the regular activity at the facility; every time Don or a member of his family arrived at the warehouse to pick up yet another new

When Don Richards bought this International Harvester B614 and its partner from a tractor wrecker, they had already been rescued from two other scrapyards, but they had never been restored.

This B614, serial number XB622, was a one-off prototype built for testing on Canadian farms in a modified "Western Special" version. It was the only one ever built.

machine to be sold on their lot, it would be impossible to miss seeing the B614s going about their work. One of the reasons Don and his family noticed these tractors is that they were the only ones of their kind in the country. IH wasn't selling anything like it in the Canadian market.

According to IH policy at the time, Don was told, the company wouldn't allow these odd-ball machines to be sold because there were no parts available for them. And having an owner irate about the company's failure to supply replacement parts for his B614 would just invite trouble and bad press. . . .

From what Don could find out, IH initially imported these two tractors for testing to see if they were suitable for North American farm duties. If they met the challenge, the B614 model would be a big brother to the B414, which was already competing for farmers' attention on dealer lots. However, something didn't work out as planned, and the two prototypes were relegated to pulling trailers around the company's plant after the field testing ended. The B614 was never added to IH's Canadian lineup.

Initially, B614s were painted in the standard red-and-white livery common to the International line, but eventually the tractors were seen running around the Hamilton grounds wearing a coat of federal yellow. It seems the tractors were repainted by the maintenance staff at the plant in a color that better suited their semi-industrial use.

In the early 1970s, Don and the rest of the Richards family started becoming involved in the tractor-collecting hobby, and needless to say, they focused on collecting

International Harvesters. At about the same time, the two yellow B614s disappeared from the IH plant. On one of his trips to the dock warehouse, Don made some inquiries about the B614s and was told they had been scrapped.

According to IH policy at the time, Don was told, the company wouldn't allow these odd-ball machines to be sold because there were no parts available for them. And having an owner irate about the company's failure to supply replacement parts for his B614 would just invite trouble and bad press, even if it was the only one in the country. So the tractors fell victim to some IH company workers wielding sledge hammers, who were ordered to destroy vital parts such as the injector pump and engine block. That way no one could ever put the machines to use. After their unceremonious pounding, the pair of tractors was sent off to a Hamilton wrecking yard.

Yet IH didn't count on someone scavenging through the yard and finding the B614s. A tractor enthusiast from Niagara Falls found the battered pair, bought them, and hauled them home. His plan was apparently to fix up the two tractors someday. Unfortunately, they sat under a protective tarp in his yard for nearly thirty years, and eventually they became part of the estate his relatives had to dispose of after his death.

For the second time, the tractors found themselves headed to a scrapyard, this time in Welland, Ontario. When the tractors were being loaded onto a truck for the trip, the workers didn't see the need to handle them with any particular care. After all, they were just lumps of scrap metal. Consequently, they were further damaged in the process.

When they arrived at the Welland scrapyard, they again proved to be items someone was interested in. A local resident saw them sitting there and bought them for their tires. Unbelievably, they had escaped the crusher again. Once the tires were removed from the hulks, their new owner had no further use for them, so he sold them to a tractor wrecker in 2001.

As fate would have it, this wrecker was a friend of the Richards. He knew of their passion for collectible IH tractors, so he placed a call to Don asking if he was interested in buying a pair of B614s. "That didn't take long to answer; of course we were," Don said.

He soon had the two tractors home, but their condition was pretty bad. Time, sledge hammers, and careless crane operators had taken their toll on the unique twins. When they took stock of just exactly what they had, the Richards found the two tractors had a few differences. One, serial number B663, had 38-inch rear wheels and a three-point hitch. The other, serial number XB622, had 30-inch wheels and no three-point hitch. Number XB622, Don discovered, was likely built in IH's Doncaster, England, plant as a modified Western version of the B614.

Through his connections at IH, Don learned that the B614 tractors had high-speed steering problems, and, more notably, they were difficult to start in the cold weather—a real drawback for a tractor in Canada's climate. Those two factors may have been the reason the Canadian B614 project was cancelled, and the steering problems may have

With everyone at the Richards family's IH dealership pitching in, XB622 was restored using components from both wrecks, along with many other parts gathered from across North America and England.

been the reason the tractors were retired early from their jobs at the Hamilton plant.

Don decided that it might be possible to rebuild one tractor with parts from the two. Because XB622 was a one-off, that one got the nod for restoration. Even with the two tractors, rebuilding one tractor would require Don and his family to locate a wide variety of parts, including an engine block, manifold, and oil filter base. And getting any parts for a tractor never distributed in North America was going to be a tall order.

Fortunately, Don found an entry on the Red Power discussion forum—an internet site devoted to IH tractors—that gave him a lead on some parts. A posting from someone in England mentioned finding a radiator for an IH 634. The 634 and 614 were very similar models, so Don sent a message to the author of the posting. The two began to correspond.

Mike Waterhouse, a fellow IH enthusiast who lived in England, was the one who wrote about finding the rare radiator. Almost immediately, he was able to help with Don's parts quest. Mike already had an old filter base, and he soon located some hood decals. A friend of his was traveling from England to Canada to attend a plowing match near Don's home and brought those parts with him. Meanwhile, Mike continued scouting for some of the other parts Don needed.

The work on the restoration started even before all the parts had been found. Members of Don's crew at the dealership were able to lend their expertise in dealing with International tractors, but none had ever worked on a B614.

So the progress was a little slow at the start, as everyone delved into unfamiliar territory with the one-off tractor.

The mechanics found that at least one part from the smaller B414, which was sold in Canada, was interchangeable with the B614: The grille insert was the same. The dealership still had a new one in stock that Don had been saving for just such an occasion. Don's brother, Jim, found a wrecking yard in the United States that still had some 634 parts in stock that would also fit the B614.

When they couldn't find a useable engine block, one of Don's crew decided to take a look at one of the blocks they already had. It had a five-inch sledge-hammer hole in it, but a section of an old Farmall A block was cut out and welded into the hole in the B614 block in a skillful piece of work. The repair was a success. Don's brother also managed to find an injection pump off of a British-built IH crawler.

Finally, XB622 was ready. After more than thirty years, stays in two scrapyards, and a tractor wrecker's yard, the B614 beat the odds and fired to life in the shop of a Canadian IH dealership, the one place where it was never supposed to be. "It probably looks better now than when it was new," Don said.

Although members of the Richards family have sold many IH tractors since 1929, they're not likely to ink a deal on the B614 anytime soon. "This was a lengthy and difficult restoration," Don said. "But because of the history of this tractor—and our own nostalgia from seeing these tractors at the Hamilton plant—we felt it was important to preserve it."

Scrapyard Titan

Arnold Helgeson has a whole farmyard full of old tractors and implements—so many that his friends and neighbors sometimes think he's operating an informal museum. So when a friend saw a machine in need of rescue, he thought of Arnold.

"A friend told me there was [a tractor] in the scrapyard ready to go to the steel mill," Arnold said about the tip that led him to his rare 1916 Titan 10-20.

Arnold knew the owner of the scrapyard in the nearby town of Strasbourg, Saskatchewan, and he had heard of people making similar rescues from his steel pile before. This dealer purchased any scrap steel he could find from local residents and then shipped off everything to a local steel mill for recycling. At the time, "A lot of guys were hauling in old machinery and tractors to clean up their yards," Arnold said.

Arnold also knew that, on occasion, the good-natured owner of the steel yard would agree to barter for something someone wanted to take out of his yard. If someone saw something in the yard—like an old tractor—that he

Found in a scrap-metal depot, this 10-20 Titan was rescued by Arnold Helgeson. He paid $50 to the dealer to compensate him for the tractor's scrap-metal value. Of course, the Titan looks a little better now than it did then.

> Even though the tractor wasn't entirely complete, what there was looked to be in reasonably good condition. By any standard, $50 was beyond a bargain for a restorable Titan.

wanted, he could just bring in an equivalent amount of scrap steel and take it home.

When Arnold saw the Titan, he easily convinced the scrapyard owner to let him take it. "I paid about fifty dollars for it; that was the scrap value," Arnold said.

Because the tractor had recently been hauled in, there wasn't much debris to clear out to get it ready to load. Using the winch on his son's four-wheel-drive Scout, Arnold eased the old tractor up onto a borrowed flat-deck trailer for the trip home. "It's a pretty heavy tractor," he said. Nonetheless, the little Scout managed to pull it onto the trailer.

Even though the tractor wasn't entirely complete, what there was looked to be in reasonably good condition. By any standard, $50 was beyond a bargain for a restorable Titan. The tractor had one obvious shortcoming: The front axle was missing.

Not surprisingly, the engine was seized, and the crankshaft wouldn't turn at all. But by simply spraying penetrating oil into the cylinders, Arnold eventually broke the pistons free after some hand cranking on the flywheel. Although twisting the flywheel crank on an engine that couldn't possibly start posed no risk, other than the possibility of a few strained muscles, the manner in which the crank fits to the flywheel of the Titan is a design that Arnold doesn't consider to be very safe. If the engine backfires, he says, the flywheel counter rotates and the spinning crank that is attached to it can cause a pretty severe injury. And according to many, the Titans have a reputation for doing just that.

In fact, Arnold claims to know of a memorable incident that occurred as a result of just such a misfire. Apparently, a farmer decided to start a similar Titan during harvest many years ago. Instead of going through the trouble of cranking the flywheel by hand, the enterprising fellow wound a rope around it and tied the other end to a horse. He then had the horse pull forward to rotate the flywheel. However, the engine misfired, causing the flywheel to spin backwards, ripping the harness right off the stunned horse. Arnold didn't know how long it took the farmer to catch the panicked horse again after that!

Flywheels aside, Arnold's Titan still didn't have the means to stand on its own—not without front wheels. Again, a tip-off was the key to finding what he needed. One of Arnold's neighbors had gone to preview something at a local farm auction sale. By coincidence, he noticed what he thought was the frame of an old Titan tractor among the scrap metal that was going to be sold on sale day. He knew Arnold was restoring his own scrapyard Titan and needed a front axle, so he called right away with news about his find.

The remains were, indeed, that of a Titan. It appeared that at some point the owner had decided to sell off parts of the old machine. What remained was left to rust away in some corner of the yard, not to be seen again until it was dragged out to sell as scrap in the auction sale along with other castoffs.

When Arnold saw the hulk, it was a tailor-made solution to his restoration problem. Not only were the front axle and wheels there, but the rear ones were there, as well. That left a few spare parts—just in case.

Once again, Arnold only had to bid the amount equal to the scrap value of the steel to get the Titan chassis and parts.

After getting the parts home and installing the front axle, Arnold could now begin in earnest on getting the Titan back into working order. Early on in the process, the carburetor and governor had to be removed for overhauls. Fortunately, a friend of Arnold's had the expertise to handle those jobs. He even fabricated some replacement parts for the carb to get it functioning again.

Now, with the Titan nearly ready to start again for the first time in who knows how long, Arnold wants to avoid hand cranking the flywheel for the initial startup. He has a plan to deal with the dangerous flywheel crank, at least until he knows the magneto is firing when it should and there'll be no danger of an out-of-control crank causing injury. He'll use another tractor with a belt pulley to spin the flywheel. Local horses will, no doubt, be glad to hear that they'll be excused from that job!

CHAPTER THREE

Steam Power

A Walk in the Woods

Most tractor guys feel right at home with the smell of diesel exhaust, but there are a select few who prefer a more discerning scent: the smell of burning wood. They are the steam traction engine buffs. In 2004, I attended a vintage tractor pull in Regina, Saskatchewan, and when Clarence Hoffman's 1917 George White steamer took its turn at the drag sled, that exhaust smell—more reminiscent of a wood stove in a summer cottage—seemed strangely out of place.

Clarence has always been a fan of steam power. He was bitten by the steam bug back in the 1930s, when he fondly remembers rushing home after school to his family's farm to watch the threshing gangs harvest grain. Steamers were still widely used as the motive power for threshing machines back then, and the young boy's fascination with those puffing, lumbering behemoths eventually found an outlet when Clarence proudly took ownership of his George White in 1977.

Finding a steam traction engine to call his own took Clarence down some unexpected paths. Because of the rarity of working steam engines these days, "steam guys get to know the other [steam] fellas," Clarence said. He used that network to start his hunt to buy a steam tractor. Yet even with the inside track, it wouldn't be an easy search. Steamers have long been rare birds.

One of those steam guys who did have a traction engine he was thinking about selling was Bill McIntosh, who lived near Clarence in the town of Whitewood, Saskatchewan. Bill owned a small George White that he ran regularly. Unlike the larger steamers built early on in the steam traction era, the smaller George White that Bill owned was a late-model version that ran at a lower operating pressure, and that meant the boiler thickness was thinner and the tractor weighed much less. "They eventually found that lower boiler pressure didn't make that much difference to the power," Clarence said. And the lighter footprint made the George White much easier to handle.

When Clarence approached Bill McIntosh about buying the tractor in 1976, it seemed as though Bill was interviewing prospective buyers as if they were suitors proposing marriage. Only those with the most honorable intentions would receive the hand of Bill's prized steamer.

Clarence Hoffman's 1917 George White steam traction engine has competed in many tractor-pull events. Incredibly, the steamer has never been restored or rebuilt.

"He told me there were a lot of collectors after this engine," Clarence said. Many, it seemed, wanted to buy the George White as an investment that would eventually be moved on for a profit. There wasn't much chance they would ever get the nod from Bill, though. "I told him that if I got a hold of one, it wasn't going to go anywhere," Clarence said. Still, Bill wasn't in any rush to make a decision, so Clarence moved on.

Later that year, Clarence received a call from a friend who said he had learned of the location of two abandoned steam engines. The news seemed to have the ring of a slot machine hitting the jackpot. The engines were located in the Porcupine Forest district in northern Saskatchewan, a few hours' drive north, but they definitely wouldn't be easy to get to. Undaunted, Clarence and his son, Blaine, made the trip up to have a look at the steamers in the chilly November weather.

These two engines, a small Case and a 25-75 Garr-Scott, had been converted to skid units with their wheels removed. They had been the muscle for a sawmill operation in the remote wilderness location. Because the engines didn't need to move around after they were positioned at the mill, there was no need to keep them on wheels. "They were easier to service that way," Clarence said.

Getting to these two machines meant traveling well off the beaten path. The engines had been left in their original positions for years and were now well hidden in the forest, which had grown up around them. After following a series of logging roads, Clarence and Blaine found themselves on the edge of a lake. From there, they continued on foot. Following the directions provided to them, the pair set off into the unfamiliar landscape amid thick stands of spruce trees.

After a considerable amount of time in the bush, they eventually found themselves lost with daylight running out. They decided to abandon the search for the engines and head back. But after walking for quite some time, they found they had only traveled in a circle, ending up at the point they changed direction and attempted to find their way back to the lake. Trying for the second time, they decided to follow their first circular path, but expand the radius of the circle in hopes of finding the lake. That didn't work either, and for the second time they were back where they started.

Remembering that the lake was downhill, the two set out again, this time deciding to only walk downhill. Making their way in the moonlight, they finally emerged from the forest at the water's edge, much to their relief. They were still some distance from their car. Not surprisingly, they decided to leave the steamer search for another time and headed home, thankful to be safe and warm.

Clarence wasn't about to let that experience deter him, and by keeping in touch with his contact, he learned that in midwinter a new logging road had been bulldozed into the forest that went right past the two engines. Finding them would now be much simpler, as would the prospect of getting them hauled out.

In the early spring, Clarence returned to the Porcupine Forest area and drove up the new logging road, only to find the bulldozer operator who built the road had decided it was easier to bulldoze the two steamers aside than go around them. Consequently, they were destroyed—a heartbreaking, and seemingly needless, waste.

Some time later, the engines were scavenged for scrap steel, with only a few remnants left scattered about from the once-proud machines.

Shortly thereafter, out of the blue, Bill McIntosh unexpectedly called Clarence and offered him the George White, almost a year after Clarence offered to purchase it. Apparently, Clarence had become the successful suitor. After making the deal, Clarence soon found himself making the circuit of antique tractor shows and threshing bees with his new steamer.

The George White was built in Canada at the company's works in London, Ontario, and then assembled at a plant in Brandon, Manitoba. Although few records remain from the company that ceased building steamers around 1920—after gasoline-powered tractors took the market by storm—Clarence has reached some conclusions about his steam traction engine. Because of the engine's design and the inclusion of parts that were designed for other, larger models, it's likely that his traction engine was one of the last ones assembled in Brandon. With the company ceasing production due to rapidly declining demand, the last few models built there were assembled from remaining stocks of parts to clear out the plant.

Whether those assumptions are true or not, one of the things that can be said for this tractor is that it is one of the few models that has run continuously for nearly ninety years without restoration.

Family Traditions

To say Jack Beamish of Hamiota, Manitoba, has steam in his veins would be an understatement. "We were the last ones in this area to use steam, up until 1942," he said of the tractors in use on his family's farm. Then, surprisingly, Jack's father and uncle decided to get back into steam in the 1950s, when everyone else had already moved on to gas- and diesel-powered tractors.

Since then, wanting to have steam traction engines on the Beamish farm has become a family tradition. Jack remembers that as a boy, his father and uncle always discussed their favorite kind of tractors. "Steam: That's all they ever talked about," he said. "I guess some of it rubbed off on me."

One of those old steam memories that sticks with Jack to this day is a screening of historical films in the community hall in the small town of Hamiota, where he grew up. The steam engines breaking prairie sod in the films caught his attention like a vice, and one of the tractors featured in those old movies was a large Case 110. The Case was a giant in its time, and it certainly made an impression on young Jack. "After watching those movies, I never forgot that I was going to build a 110, no matter what," he said.

Eventually, steam engines were replaced by modern machines on the Beamish farm for the second time, and the only traces left of the steam were in the family photo album. But in the 1970s, still with vivid memories of watching those movies of the 110 Case, Jack decided he missed the hissing and puffing of those lumbering old machines. Unfortunately, he discovered, like so many others, that steam engines were now hard to find.

Building one steamer out of the parts of many that were now derelict seemed like the only affordable route, so he kept his ear to the ground for parts. When a collection of Case steam traction parts turned up on the sale bill of an auction to be held in Iowa, Jack made the long trip and bought everything he could get his hands on. Even with his new pile of old parts, he was still far from his dream of having an operating engine.

In 1977, that dream became a lot closer to reality when he caught wind of a boiler and undercarriage that were for sale near Prince George in central British Columbia, more than 1,200 miles away. If he could get the boiler and undercarriage, he would finally have the basis of a steamer that he could begin to turn into a working tractor. The boiler was being sold by a paving company that had used it for heating road tar until Jack found it. Before that, it had been a skid unit used for power at a sawmill. The paving company bought it in 1963 and put it to work on highway construction.

Jack Beamish's farmyard looks like it could be the back lot of a steam-engine manufacturing plant near the turn of the twentieth century. A wide assortment of parts, ranging from wheels to boilers, sits hiding in the grass waiting to be used on some future project.

This boiler for a Model 110 Case was found at an abandoned sawmill in northern Manitoba. It was hauled out of the wilderness and across a frozen lake during the winter, but it needed significant repairs before it could be put back to use.

Sitting among a collection of parts and old tractors, this 45-horsepower Case is a work in progress. Like all of Jack Beamish's tractors, it is made up of parts that have been collected from all across North America.

Jack and his son, Colin, have restored at least one example of all of the steam traction engines ever offered by J. I. Case. They may be the only restorers able to make that claim.

Yes, getting the 110 finished was no small job. "It took thousands of hours, just thousands and thousands. . . ."

Jack had had an incredible stroke of good luck in finding the boiler. Not only was the boiler in good condition, but it was from a 110-horsepower Case, his favorite brand and model of steamer, just like the one he saw in the films all those years ago. He bought the boiler right away and had it hauled home.

Yet even after getting the boiler and adding it to the pile of parts he bought in Iowa, he still had barely 50 percent of the parts he needed to create a 110. The rest of the parts were nowhere to be found, despite his best efforts. That left him with only one option: to make what he needed. He would need to find original parts to make casts from and get a foundry to make one-off parts at a reasonable cost. That was a tall order in itself, and all of that had to be accomplished while running the family farm and working as a power engineer at a local electrical generating station in the nearby city of Brandon. Jack found himself spending every free hour in the workshop. "I'd work until five a.m., get three hours sleep, and get up at eight to go to work," he said.

A further stroke of good luck helped with getting parts cast. Another local steam enthusiast also needed some of the same parts and happened to have some molds he was willing to share with Jack. Eventually, the two men found a small network of enthusiasts with similar parts needs.

"Making parts was a team effort," Jack said. Originally, a foundry in Fargo, North Dakota, cast the parts for them. When the foundry closed, the group was forced to look elsewhere. Another foundry in Webster, North Dakota, closer to the Canadian border, took up the slack, and the enthusiasts continued with their projects.

The biggest undertaking in building parts for the Case was in making the rear axle castings. Jack and two others all needed the part. Each single casting weighed about 600 pounds and cost a staggering $3,000, proving to Jack that the steam hobby was going to require some deep pockets.

Yes, getting the 110 finished was no small job. "It took thousands of hours, just thousands and thousands," Jack said. All of that work took place over the course of six years, and in 1982, the 110 was finally ready to fire up.

Researching the origins of his tractor turned up some interesting facts. Originally, the 110 boiler and undercarriage were sold new in 1913 in Edmonton, Alberta. When the assembly left the J. I. Case plant in 1911, it was part of an original prairie 110 steam traction engine, designed for a variety of farming uses. Only later was it converted to a skid unit for the sawmill. No one knows now where the remaining original pieces went when the traction engine was partly dismantled for its modified duty at the sawmill.

"Case[s] were the best-designed tractors for plowing," Jack said. And he thinks the Case models were an all-

A trip to an old sawmill site in the Porcupine Forest district of northern Saskatchewan turned up a wide variety of parts, which included the engine on this 65 Case. While just walking through the tall grass, Jack literally stumbled over the rear wheels now in use on this traction engine.

around superior design, as well. The rear-mount engines made servicing them much easier than many of the other brands. And the 110 was the flagship of that steam-tractor line; it offered a locomotive cab and, incredibly, power steering. That's not an option that comes to mind when one thinks of steam traction engines, or even early gasoline-powered ones.

Now Jack has an unbelievable nine Case steam tractors in his collection. All of them have required some amount of manufacturing to turn into complete, working machines. Still, that hasn't stopped Jack from adding to his fleet of steamers. The first steamers came to Jack's family farm in the early 1900s, when his grandfather had a threshing operation with steam-tractor power that traveled around the countryside threshing grain every fall with a crew of twenty-five men. Now, the steamers on Jack's farm just perform for the occasional crowd of admirers during antique agricultural events, or when Jack decides to power up his old sawmill. Obviously, all those evenings spent listening to his father and uncle talk about the good old days of steam left their mark on Jack. As long as he has the family farm, there will be talk of the glory of steam around the kitchen table, just like all those many years ago.

Across the Ice

Murray Johanson of Langruth, Manitoba, had just completed restoring a 1916 Case 75 steam engine and was already looking for another project to work on. During a casual conversation with another steam-engine enthusiast, Murray asked the fateful question: "Do you think a guy could get enough parts together to build a 110?"

That was in 1994, and the answer to his question led him to Pat Nicholson. Pat had a cache of parts for a 110 Case that had been discovered nearly thirty years prior, in 1966. After nearly three decades, the parts had still not been reassembled—an astounding fact considering the amount of work that went into finding and recovering the remains of the engine. Pat found what was left of the 110 on an island in the center of Lake Winnipegosis in north-central Manitoba, at the site of an abandoned sawmill. The 110, it seems, had been bought for use at the remote mill. At the time, steam traction engines were falling out of favor with farmers, due to the upstart internal-combustion-engine tractors. That made the steamers cheap power sources, ideal for use at sawmills where fuel was free and plentiful.

Getting them into these remote locations where there were few, if any, roads was no easy chore. Some were stripped down and hauled into the isolated mills across frozen winter roads. Once the sawmills ceased operations some years later, it was just too expensive to haul the old engines back out again, especially considering there was no longer any real demand for steam power. That made those old engines worth only as much as their steel would bring at a recycling depot; certainly, that wasn't enough to justify the cost of their transportation.

Eventually, steam enthusiasts, like Pat Nicholson, began scouring the northern forests for the remains of these old machines. Pat came to the island in Lake Winnipegosis to check out the 110 and three other smaller engines that had been abandoned. With the help of a local guide, Pat made a boat trip across the lake to visit the old sawmill site and see for himself what remained. The 110 boiler was still there, but it had been stripped down. Luckily, a lot of the parts were still strewn about the old mill site. The removal effort began by gathering up the smaller pieces and hauling them back across the lake by boat. But the boiler and differential unit were simply too large for that; they would have to stay put until winter set in.

Once the ice was thick enough to support a vehicle, all the boilers were loaded onto sleighs and skidded across the frozen lake to the mainland. After the remains of all the old engines were brought across, they were left at a small community on the shore until spring arrived and the machines could be loaded and hauled to Pat's farmstead. The collection made its home at Pat's for

> Once the inspection was complete, the results were devastating. After all the effort required to bring the boiler from the island in 1966 and now to Murray's farm, the reading showed the walls had degraded and were too thin for it to safely operate.

years, and many collectors tried to persuade him to sell off the gigantic pile of steam-engine parts, but to no avail. Nevertheless, Murray decided he would make the fifty-mile trip to Pat's farm and see what the chances were of him getting the 110 components.

The old expression "timing is everything" held true for Murray. Pat had finally decided that he wasn't going to be the person to rebuild the 110, even though his dream was to see it reassembled. If it was going to happen, someone else would have to do it. Not long after Pat reached that conclusion, Murray drove up his driveway. Before Pat was willing to shake on the deal, he needed to find out a little bit about who this potential new owner really was. So he asked around and did a little research to determine if Murray was a reliable sort and to find out what kind of experience he had with traction engines. Finally, Murray was given the seal of approval, and Pat announced he was willing to let the 110 go. There was one condition: Murray would get the parts only on the understanding that he would create a working 110 tractor from them.

When the parts finally arrived at Murray's, the first job was to catalog everything and find out what condition things were really in. After that was completed, the next step was to get an ultrasound examination done on the boiler. Once the inspection was complete, the results were devastating. After all the effort required to bring the boiler from the island in 1966 and now to Murray's farm, the reading showed the walls had degraded and were too thin for it to safely operate. The project was scuttled, even before it had really started.

With uncertainty now surrounding the 110 project, the only way forward would be to get another boiler—but from where? Murray's answer came from the same friend who had mentioned Pat Nicholson's name. Ken May was another steam-engine hunter who had also acquired a 110 from a northern location, this time in the neighboring province of Saskatchewan. Ken's 110 had last sawed timbers for a mine before being abandoned and coming back to civilization in much the same way as Pat Nicholson's did. And, just like Pat, Ken had his boiler and parts sitting unrestored for some time. So Murray went to see him.

After convincing Ken that his 110 boiler and parts would be put to good use, Murray got the nod once again to take home the Case pieces. His first order of business was to get a detailed examination of this boiler's condition. This time, all was well; the boiler was useable. Finally, after the Nicholson and May 110 collections had spent years in storage, they would now be blended into one working traction engine.

Over the next two years, parts were either refurbished in Murray's own shop or by specialist machinists. By the end of 1996, all the parts were repaired or restored to like-new condition, and the traction engine was ready for reassembly. The following January, reassembly started in the workshop on Murray's farm. On July 25, 1999, the 110 created out of the remains of two fired to life for the first time, watched by many of the machinists and other steam enthusiasts who helped Murray find the pieces or create it.

When you buy a new tractor, you get the key handed to you with a little pomp and ceremony, and the same held true for Murray and his wife, Linda, who had a special "key" to the 110 Case presented to them by their friends. In their case, the key to their steam traction engine was a firebox poker!

Up the River
without a Barge

Wayne Fischer had been interested in steam power since he was a kid and always dreamed of someday owning his own traction engine. Finally after thinking about making that dream come true, he went to Indiana to take a steam traction engine operator's course—to learn how to use one first. On returning from that course in 1999, he walked into a store that sold working steam models and bought a model of a 75 Case engine. "I thought someday I would buy an engine and hoped it would be one just like that," Wayne said.

The following year, he put the word out that he was looking to finally buy his own engine. That soon paid dividends. A friend called and told him a steam enthusiast named John McKay was selling an engine, and it was a 75 Case, just like the model Wayne wanted. Wayne called John and started the negotiation process. The 1912 Model 75 Case and John's other engine, a 1913 76-horsepower Sawyer-Massey, were booked into a steam show that

The perilous barge trip down the Pickerel River that nearly saw the 75 Case end up on the river bottom was recorded by Allan Byers on his 8-millimeter film camera. If only all old tractor rescues were so completely documented! Wayne Fisher was given the film when he bought the last engine in Allan Byers' collection.

At the end of the voyage, the Case and the John Deere bulldozer were readied for offroading. A low-bed trailer was backed up to the barge and the engine was pushed onto it for the final leg of the trip down the Trans-Canada Highway. The man on the barge is one of the crew members who worked to bring the engine out of the forest.

summer at St. Thomas, Ontario. Wayne went to the show and had a chance to see the Case at work.

The two made a deal on the engine, but Wayne had to wait until after another steam working expo later in the season, where the Case was already booked to perform. Attending that second show gave Wayne a chance to get behind the wheel and learn how to run the old engine before getting it home. Eventually, Wayne bought John's Sawyer-Massey and his eight-bottom plow, as well as the Case. During one of their conversations, John told Wayne about the history of all those machines and where they were before John acquired them. With a little more digging, Wayne was able to piece together a pretty complete history of his 75 Case—one that turned out to be somewhat surprising and colorful.

The engine was built in 1912 for export to Canada, where boiler regulations at the time were a little more stringent than in the United States. As a result, it had a Canadian Special boiler design. The engine was delivered to a dealer in Winnipeg, Manitoba, and sold in 1913. The traction engine spent years at work in prairie farm fields and then sat idle until it attracted the attention of a sawmill owner from Ontario.

After the sawmill owner bought the engine, it was loaded onto a Canadian Pacific Railway flat car and, accompanied by a crane, was sent to a remote forest location in Ontario. In order to get the engine to the right place, the train hauling it had to make a special stop along the rail line where the track crosses the Pickerel River. From the railway bridge, the traction engine was unchained, lifted by the crane, and lowered onto the ground near the river bank. From there, it was fired up and driven a little farther into the forest to the sawmill site. It stayed in this wilderness, powering the mill's saw, until the area was logged out about six or seven years later. Then, once again, it sat idle, but now it was stranded by the remoteness of the mill site. Nonetheless, the mill's owner had a plan to cash in on it.

In 1960, needing a bulldozer to work at logging jobs in another forested area, the engine's owner made a trip to a John Deere construction equipment dealer near Orillia, Ontario. The owner of that dealership, Allan Byers, was a steam enthusiast and was always on the lookout for more engines for his collection. So when the Case's owner offered the engine as down payment on a new bulldozer, Allan agreed.

It seems, though, that the sawmill owner didn't expect anyone to be able to actually get the engine out of its current, nearly inaccessible, location. A few days after making the deal, Allan Byers was talking to another man who told him he, too, had bought a 75 Case and described its location. That sounded an awful lot like the engine Allan just agreed to take as a trade-in.

Suspecting the sawmill owner had sold the engine twice, Allan took quick action to secure his investment. He put together a crew and rented a lumber barge to make the trip up the Pickerel River to recover the Case before someone else did. By now, the newly constructed Trans-Canada Highway was only a mile or so downriver from the railway bridge where the Case was offloaded in 1947. So, if the engine could be loaded onto a barge and floated

The 75 Case rode into Allan Byers' yard on the bed of a truck. Notice the wood bunkers at the back of the engine have been removed. They would eventually be replaced by reproduction pieces.

downriver, it could be loaded onto a truck and easily hauled the remaining distance back to Orillia.

Barely a week after making the deal on the Case, Allan and his crew beached their rented barge on the riverbank near the railway bridge and drove off with a bulldozer from the dealership, which was brought along to provide some muscle. With the dozer, they built a causeway that would allow the engine to be pushed up onto the barge's deck once it was towed down to the shore by the crawler. The men expected to get the engine out with just a day's work, and initially, everything was going to plan. They found the engine, towed it back with the crawler, and pulled it up onto the barge. Once the Case and the dozer were secured on the deck, the barge was then towed out into the stream. Then things got a little scary. The barge was top-heavy and began rocking wildly in the choppy water. "They almost lost the engine and the bulldozer," Wayne said.

In a desperate attempt to avoid a disaster, they beached the barge back at the original loading site. All breathed a great sigh of relief at being safely back on dry land. Aside from the obvious risk of possibly drowning the crew, it would have been a shame to lose the Case after so much time, effort, and money had already been spent trying to retrieve it, not to mention the chance of losing the dozer, too.

After considering how to next proceed, the crew members decided that they needed another barge. By tying two together, they thought they could stabilize them. So some of the crew went back downriver to rent a second barge, while the remaining men went to work cutting down some strong trees that they planned to use to lash the two vessels together. Essentially, the second barge would be attached to one side, like the pontoon on a Polynesian canoe.

When the second barge arrived and the two were secured to each other, Allan Byers and his crew made another attempt to navigate downstream. This time, the two barges floated easily with the engine and bulldozer firmly chained to the deck. By the time they reached the offloading point near the highway, the evening light was fading; work had to be suspended for the day. The following morning, the bulldozer and traction engine came off the barge and were loaded onto a truck for the landlocked portion of the trip back to Orillia.

Allan's quick action in getting the Case hauled out of its wilderness home ensured his sizeable investment in the old engine was protected. No one now seems to know what came of the second possible sale. Maybe the mill owner was right, and the daunting task facing anyone wanting to get the engine back to civilization made it unlikely anyone else ever tried, even if there really was a second deal.

Because the Case had only been sitting idle a relatively short few years, it was still in fine working order. Only the wood bunkers on the rear had been removed. These bunkers had a reputation for prematurely rusting out. That meant many Case traction engines often were found without their bunkers in place. "They were just made of sheet metal. They didn't last," Wayne said. For that reason, reproduction bunkers were commonly available.

After Allan Byers died, Wayne learned that the last remaining engine in his estate was up for sale. Allan's son, Rob, apparently hadn't inherited his father's passion for steam. Because the Case, the Sawyer-Massey, and the eight-bottom plow Wayne bought from John McKay had all been part of Allan's collection at one time, having the remaining engine would see that collection reunited. So Wayne gave Rob Byers a call. Although a tentative deal was pending with another buyer, Rob seemed pleased at the idea of seeing his father's collection back together in one place. He changed his plans and sold the remaining engine to Wayne.

On the day of the final transaction, Wayne made the trip to Rob's home and arrived early in the morning. Rob greeted him at the door and motioned for Wayne to follow him down into the basement of the house. Downstairs, Wayne and Rob walked into a room where the curtains

The 75 Case was eventually restored by its current owner, Wayne Fischer. After learning how to operate steam traction engines, Wayne decided he wanted a 75 Case, and only one year later, he bought this one.

were drawn and there was an eight-millimeter film projector set up. Rob turned out the lights and flicked on the projector. Wayne could hardly believe his eyes when he saw the film. Allan, it turns out, had the foresight to document the perilous barge trip with an old eight-millimeter movie camera. The film showed the Case and the smaller bulldozer floating down the Pickerel River on that day in October 1960. The film's box still had the cancelled postage on it, which read "November 1960," the date Allan mailed the film to the processing lab.

After turning the lights back on and rewinding the film, Rob handed Wayne the box of film and said he could have it now that he owned Allan's former steam collection. The film seems to be as much a part of the steam-powered collection as the engines themselves.

Wayne thought just finding out about the Case's ownership history was an achievement, but finding a film documenting its most memorable moment was icing on the cake.

So, the next time you go tractor hunting, remember to put a camera in your pocket. The pictures you take of your adventure may prove to be nearly as valuable a memento as the tractor itself. Certainly a documented history adds something irreplaceable, even if it is future generations who will reap the benefits of your efforts.

CHAPTER FOUR

The Collectors

Michigan Backyards

As a building contractor, Steve Ash gets to drive a different direction to work every couple of months. After one building project finishes, he starts a new one in another area of the countryside. Steve and his family have taken advantage of that opportunity to regularly see many different neighborhoods all across Michigan, and as a result they've found some great vintage tractors.

Having been raised on a farm, Steve has an appreciation for old iron. His father, Clare, operated the roughly 2,000-acre family farm until 1993, when he decided to retire. Clare lived on the farm for about a year after it was sold, during the transition of ownership. He still had a fully equipped workshop near his back door, but nothing to do in it. Steve tried to coax him to restore a tractor, so Clare could stay active.

In 1994, Steve was building a new house for a customer in Manistique, a town on Michigan's remote Upper Peninsula. At some point, Clare drove over to the building site, which wasn't too far from the farm, to visit with Steve and see how the work was progressing. Just as Steve and his crew were readying to set the roof trusses, an afternoon rain shower put a stop to the work. With building at a standstill, Steve and Clare decided to hop into Steve's pickup truck and take a drive around the unfamiliar neighborhood to see the sights.

During their tour, Steve noticed a large pile of old car tires in the yard of a home on a small acreage. Just barely visible over the top of the tire pile was the exhaust pipe and hood of an old tractor. For curiosity's sake, Steve stopped the truck, and he and his father strained to determine what model of tractor was hiding just out of sight. The classic green color gave away its brand. It was a John Deere, but all they could tell was that it was an old one.

Steve suggested that working on an old John Deere might be the perfect project for Clare now that he had free time on his hands. Clare agreed, and the two decided to see if the owner would consider selling the mystery tractor. Steve pulled the truck into the driveway of the house, and Clare went to the front door to speak to the owner. He was home and appeared at the door within seconds. However, he wasn't too receptive to the idea of parting with the old tractor. He was going to fix it up one day, he said. That day

This 1940 John Deere unstyled Model BR was nearly hidden from the road by a pile of old tires that had accumulated in this backyard over the years. The tractor was missing its cylinder head and one piston.

just hadn't arrived yet. Nevertheless, he allowed Steve and Clare to walk back behind the mountain of tires and have a look at the old machine for themselves.

It was a 1940 unstyled Model BR, and it needed a lot more than just TLC. The head had been removed from the engine, and it was clear that the tractor had been sitting that way for quite some time. On top of that, only one piston was left in the block. The tires still held air, but only barely. Nearby was another unstyled Deere, but it looked much worse than the BR. In spite of its problems, Clare saw some potential in the BR. So he left the owner his phone number and an offer, just in case the owner decided to change his mind.

The BR is nearly unrecognizable from its former appearance after undergoing a complete restoration. The work couldn't be completed, however, until another Model B was found that could be purchased as a parts donor.

That tactic paid off about a week later when the owner of the BR called Clare and asked if he was still interested in the old tractor. The two cinched a deal. Using a sixteen-foot, flat-deck trailer from Steve's worksite, the two headed back in Steve's pickup to get the old Deere. After loading it, they hauled it back to Clare's farmyard and put it into the workshop.

A thorough inspection revealed just what condition the BR was really in. By applying liberal amounts of WD40 and a lot of elbow grease, Steve was able to help his father free the stuck piston and get the crankshaft to turn by repeatedly twisting the flywheel back and forth. The rest of the tractor was in reasonably good condition, despite looking its age.

Another back road drive through the town of Gulliver, Michigan, turned up a Model B that was well beyond repair, but it did have the parts that that were missing from the BR. Fortunately, this owner was also willing to sell, so the B was hauled back to Clare's workshop where the required parts were transplanted onto the BR.

Once the missing engine parts were grafted onto the old BR and all the mechanical problems had been addressed, Steve once again helped out by spraying a new coat of John Deere green over the tractor. Then he and his dad carefully applied its new decals.

The unstyled BR, it seems, touched off a restoration spark in Clare. This Deere would be only the first of many more tractors that Steve's father would bring back from the brink of scrap-metal status. So far, Clare, along with some occasional help from his family, has fully restored an average of one tractor a year since he finished the BR. As any restorer will attest, that's an impressive rate of productivity.

The Silver King

By 2002, Clare had several tractor projects under his belt, and his two sons were now his eyes and ears when it came to scouting potential new projects. That year, Clare's other son, Denni, was the one to bring home some interesting tractor news. Denni's job, working for a company that cleared brush away from utility lines in Michigan, allowed him to see a lot of country from an uncommon perspective. Following the routes of electrical utility lines took Denni in, around, and behind much of Michigan's countryside.

One day while going about his routine, Denni noticed a unique collection of old tractors, cars, and various antiques at the back of a nearby property, which wasn't too far from the town of Strongs. When time finally allowed, Denni stopped and introduced himself to the property owner, who was an elderly gentleman. Denni mentioned being fascinated by the unusual collection of machines on the property, and the owner was more than happy to give him a guided tour of the grounds and the inside of an old barn that housed even more gems. One of the more unbelievable finds hiding on the acreage was a long, wooden bar that had once supported the elbows of thousands of saloon goers. It had been removed completely intact—an architectural historian's dream to be sure.

However, it was the tractors that Denni was interested in. He knew Clare would be more than eager to haul another tractor treasure into his workshop. One tractor caught Denni's eye, an unusual model that was definitely showing its age. Denni tested the water by asking if the owner would be willing to part with it. The answer, somewhat surprisingly, was yes.

The tractor was a 1936 Silver King, but it was no longer silver. It had been repainted in a bright industrial color that was now well-faded and spotted with rusty patches. When Denni returned home for the weekend, he called his dad

Clare Ash didn't think this tractor would run when he bought it, but he was able to start it and drive it onto the trailer for the trip home from a Michigan backyard.

and told him about the find. Not long after getting that information, Clare was on the phone and immediately made a deal on the tractor. Clare, who was by now living near Steve in southern Michigan, near Lansing, made the trip back up to Strongs in the northern part of the state to get the Silver King. He fully equipped the trailer he towed behind his truck for any eventuality when it came to loading the tractor.

After backing up to the old Silver King, Clare began getting out the chains and come-alongs he had packed to pull the tractor on board. The old fellow who sold him the tractor stood nearby and was by now quite puzzled as he watched Clare. "What are you going to do with all that?" he asked. When Clare described how he planned to winch the tractor up onto the trailer, the old fellow simply smiled and said, "Why don't you just start it up and drive it on?"

The question took Clare by surprise. Based on Denni's description, he just assumed the tractor didn't run and negotiated the deal accordingly. Finding out the tractor actually ran was an unexpected and very pleasant bonus.

After pouring some gas in it, the Silver King fired to life and dutifully pulled itself up onto the trailer.

The old tractor's strange paint job turned out to be a uniform given to it by some county or town road maintenance department. The turf-style tires and the various homemade brackets attached to it all suggested the old machine had spent much of its life cutting road ditches, or performing some other kind of maintenance duties. Marketed by their manufacturer as the first tractors ever to

Clare stands behind his now-restored 1936 Silver King. This tractor appeared to have been used for road maintenance or similar work because it was painted a bright, industrial color when it was found.

be designed from the ground up to use rubber tires, Silver Kings were popular with road maintenance authorities. Also, the Silver King's low-slung design made it stable when working along ditches. And with a top speed of 25 miles per hour, the Silver King could virtually race down the road in comparison to other agricultural tractors of the time.

Incredibly, that speed could actually increase to an unbelievable 45 miles per hour with the optional gears the company offered. Whether anyone actually ever had the nerve to drive one that fast seems to be a fair question, particularly as many rural North American roads of that era were noted for being somewhat less than perfect. As for Clare's Silver King, he's not sure how fast it will go. He hasn't found anyone willing to pilot it down a quarter-mile drag strip.

Before starting his restoration, Clare took stock of the Silver King's condition. Amazingly, the old turf tires were still fine. Once topped up with air, they were good enough to stay on the tractor. Aside from some wiring replacement, a carburetor overall, and some minor rust removal, the restoration was totally cosmetic. Steve's son sprayed a new coat of silver on the tractor, and it was ready to show. The toughest part of the whole restoration was finding a properly restored example to make sure the paint scheme Clare decided on was historically accurate.

Fate Intervenes at the County Fair

Despite the fact Jon Kinzenbaw, or Kinze as he's known to his friends, has literally hundreds of tractors in his collection, he can easily pick a favorite—his 1946 Farmall H. It is a machine his father used to own and the tractor Kinze learned to drive on. However, this tractor wasn't passed down from father to son. It only became a part of Kinze's collection after fate—coincidence, luck, or whatever you want to call it—intervened.

The Farmall H first made its home on the Kinzenbaw farm in Victor, Iowa, when Kinze's dad bought it after returning home from service in World War II. At that time, Kinze was just a toddler. The tractor was still around when young Kinze was finally given the chance to take the controls—even though he was just a bit too small to reach the clutch pedal. His father fixed that problem by attaching a large block of wood to the pedal with a hinge to bring the pedal a little closer. A piece of rubber cut from an old tire provided a nonslip surface to keep Kinze's boot from sliding off.

This basic, but clever, solution made it possible for Kinze to rack up more than a few happy hours at the wheel of the H. But eventually, his father decided he needed more horses under the hood and traded the H back to the dealer for a larger Farmall Super M. Over the years, that Farmall dealer closed up shop, and all records of the sales and trades were lost to time. So around 1983, when Kinze first started making inquiries to locate the old H, the dealer proved to be a dead-end lead. Kinze had no record of the H's serial number to help, either. In those days, keeping serial number records just didn't seem that important.

With the passage of so much time and nothing more than his recollections of a few unique features the H acquired over the years, Kinze wondered if he would ever find it. All he knew was that when it left the family farm it still had the hinge on the clutch, once mated to a block of wood, and a parking brake lever from an old Chevy truck that served as the throttle lever. In all likelihood, those parts were now long-since removed. He began to resign himself to the fact that the only place he would ever see the old H again was in his memories of the days spent working with his father on the family farm.

Kinze didn't continue on with the family tradition of farming, but he did choose a career in agriculture—running Kinze Manufacturing, which produces farm implements. The company makes a nice fit with Kinze's passion for old tractors. He is able to keep his tractor collection close to his manufacturing plant, and occasionally he draws on the mechanical expertise of some employees to help with

Rescued at virtually the last moment from being sold to a wrecker and scrapped for parts, the Farmall H that belonged to Jon Kinzenbaw's father is now fully restored and is the centerpiece of Jon's tractor collection.

Jon, or Kinze as he is known to his friends, still had the original block of wood his father had attached to the tractor decades ago to help Kinze reach the clutch pedal. The other part of the hinge was still attached to the pedal when Kinze found the tractor.

the restorations.

In 1993, Kinze helped his son with the restoration of a Cub Cadet tractor as a 4-H project. That little tractor and his son's report on the rebuilding process were entered in an Iowa county fair that year. While helping his son at the fair, it started raining, so Kinze decided to go inside and wait out the storm. As he was killing time, he began looking at some of the other children's projects. A photograph display belonging to a boy who was showing his project here rather than at the fair in his own county caught Kinze's eye.

As he stepped up for a closer look, he noticed one picture that had a familiar appearance. It was the silhouette of a Farmall H with an unusual, and noticeable, feature. Instead

Kinze's father had replaced the worn-out throttle assembly with this Chevy parking brake lever salvaged from an old truck. It was the feature that stood out and helped Kinze identify the tractor.

of a stock throttle assembly, the tractor in the picture had a lever that extended above the steering wheel. Kinze had seen that before—on his dad's H.

"It hit me like a ton of bricks. There was Dad's old H sitting in the weeds," Kinze said.

Kinze checked the name associated to the photo display and immediately began looking for Tanner, the young boy who entered the photo project. It didn't take long to find him and his father and ask them about the tractor in the picture.

As it happened, that tractor was on the family's farm across the river in Benton County, and, yes, Tanner's father said he would sell it. In fact, he had been planning to sell

"It hit me like a ton of bricks. There was Dad's old H sitting in the weeds. . . ."

it to a local wrecker for parts, but that deal wasn't finalized yet. Tanner's father said he would need about $500 to part with it. After negotiating, they settled on a price of $400.

When Kinze showed up with his trailer to get the tractor, he gave the H a once over. He knew quickly that he was looking at an old friend. After loading the H, Kinze went to the cab of his truck and returned with an old block of wood; it had some old rubber and half a hinge attached to it. He asked Tanner and his parents, who were watching from nearby, to come close and take a look. Then, he held the wooden block up to the clutch pedal, and it fit perfectly with the rusted hinge section that was still bolted to the back of the pedal. It was as certain an identification as if he had compared a fingerprint. The old Chevy brake lever, instead of the Farmall throttle, was still in place, too.

Kinze knew that, if pressed, he would have paid the full asking price for the tractor. That's part of the reason he had deliberately not told Tanner and his dad why he wanted it. Now that the deal was done, he went back to his truck, took out his checkbook, and wrote out a $100 check. This one, however, he made out to Tanner as a finder's fee.

Over the next couple of years, the H underwent a complete restoration in Kinze's shop. Although it looked a little rough around the edges when he brought it home, only the engine needed any serious repairs. Usually, Kinze only replaces the seals on the transmissions and rear ends of his tractors, unless there are other repairs required. However, this tractor was special. It also was treated to a full set of new bearings.

Just before Kinze's father traded the H, it was fitted with a new pair of Goodyear rear tires with 45-degree tread bars. Amazingly, those same tires were still on the tractor and still serviceable.

A year after buying the H, Kinze ran into Tanner's mother at the annual county fair. She had a story she just had to share with him. She said that when Tanner was thinking about what project he would create for the fair that year, he asked her this: "Mom, what do you think I could take pictures of this year that Kinze would want to buy?"

Airborne Invasion

If the military can use air power to turn the tide of a battle, can it be used to gain an advantage in negotiating the sale of an old tractor? Frank Thompson proved it can— way back in 1954.

Frank and his father, Frank Sr., farmed in southern Saskatchewan, and they were both interested in collecting old machines. Frank Sr. had a fondness for old tractors. Like many young men, Frank Jr.'s passion was for old cars.

Back in the 1950s, rural Saskatchewan was populated by many small farms, and most farmers, being practical, sensible people, had little use for outdated, obsolete equipment. The technological advances in farm tractors and automobiles of that time had people looking ahead rather than behind. "Old cars were a dime a dozen, and even more so for old tractors," Frank said. However, Frank and his father had a more visionary approach.

The province of Saskatchewan celebrated its fiftieth anniversary in 1955, and many communities had celebrations that involved old tractors that were pulled out of the bush, repaired, and used in parades and special events. After the celebrations were over, few seemed interested in doing anything with the tractors, other than letting them return to their retired status. As a result, Frank and his father didn't have to go far to find an exceptional variety of machines to add to their collections. One of those acquisitions stands out to Frank as especially memorable.

In 1954, Frank's father had his eye on a 1913 30-60 Titan, a Model TJ, that was owned by a pair of bachelor brothers who lived about ten miles away from the Thompsons' farm. The Titan had been parked in the brothers' farmyard for a very long time, and it hadn't seen any activity or attention for just as long. Despite that, the brothers seemed to have a sentimental attachment to it. It had belonged to their father, and they had flatly refused Frank Sr.'s offers to purchase it on more than one occasion. Still, Frank's father couldn't drop the idea of buying it; he really wanted to have it in his collection.

The Titan was a rare one. It was one of the few remaining examples that was equipped with an air starter. The operator first had to start a small gasoline engine, which powered an air compressor. Once sufficient air pressure was built up, the compressed air was forced into the cylinders of the main engine, spinning the crankshaft and starting the tractor.

Many tractors of the Titan's era had been gathered up and recycled for their scrap steel during World War II, but the brothers had steadfastly refused to part with theirs even if it meant not supporting the war effort. They had no desire for the old tractor to be melted down.

As part of his fascination with machines and mechanical things, Frank learned to fly and bought a Cessna 140 back in 1950. He had a few years of flying experience under his belt on the summer day in 1954 when he and his father decided to go for a leisurely flight. It was a Sunday morning and the weather was perfect for flying. As they surveyed the patchwork of farms from high in the air, the two found themselves in the vicinity of the old 30-60; Frank's father suggested they fly over the brothers' farmyard to see it from the air. So Frank slowed the engine and dropped to a lower altitude for a low-level pass.

Light aircraft were a bit of a novelty in this part of the world in the 1950s, so the fly-by drew the attention of everyone in the farmyard. People came rushing out of the house to look up and wave at the small plane. After creating an audience, Frank decided to be friendly and put the plane down for a chat with the family. A level field beside the old tractor proved to be a perfect landing strip, and the plane touched down and taxied toward the yard. "Flying into someone's farmyard for a visit was a pretty rare thing back then," Frank said.

As everyone visited, Frank asked one of the brothers if he had ever been in an airplane before. Like most rural people at that time, he hadn't. When Frank invited him to go for a ride, he didn't have to ask twice. Soon Frank and one of the brothers were high above the countryside. Frank's passenger was clearly enjoying himself as they flew over the landscape. About twenty minutes later, they were taxiing back down the field toward the farmyard, and Frank soon found himself taking off again with the other brother, who was also eager to experience flying for himself.

Frank Thompson offered the original owners of this 1913 Titan a ride in his airplane on a Sunday morning in 1954, and that trip finally convinced them to sell the tractor to his father, who was a tractor collector.

When the plane touched down after the second flight, Frank's second passenger asked if Frank and his father would wait a few minutes before leaving. He said he wanted to talk to his brother about selling the old Titan to Frank's father. It was an unexpected comment. The two brothers took a short walk away from the group and talked between themselves. They apparently considered the free airplane rides such a thoughtful act that they agreed to sell the Titan as a way of showing their gratitude.

When they came back to the plane, they announced that they would sell, and, needless to say, Frank's father was delighted. He wrote them a check on the spot; then the two

Franks hopped in the plane and headed straight home. When they arrived back at their farmyard, Frank fuelled up a D-6 crawler they had on the farm and started on a slow march to cover the ten miles down the road back to the brothers' farm to get the Titan. Frank's father and a friend went ahead and jacked up the old tractor to free it from having sunk into the ground after fifteen or twenty years of sitting in one spot. They oiled and greased it, and by the time the D-6 arrived, the Titan was ready to be pulled home.

The next day, the Titan was given a full inspection. After mostly some minor repairs, it was running for the first time in years. "It was one of the few tractors we ever bought that had to have so little done to it," Frank said.

Even though the brothers let go of the Titan, they kept close tabs on it. Eager to see it running again, they were soon over at Frank's to drive it—for old time's sake. Eventually, Frank's father decided to put on an annual show that featured the Titan, and the two brothers would always be there to help run the tractor. They didn't seem to have ever regretted their decision to sell the tractor after their first, and likely only, airplane rides.

The Titan TJ is now one of only a handful in North America, and it has had nothing more done to it than getting a new paint job and undergoing that first day of mechanical tinkering by Frank and his father. With more than eighty tractors and fifty cars in the collections amassed by the Thompsons, the Titan stands out as a symbol of times spent with two fathers: Frank with his that day in the airplane and the two brothers with theirs over part of a lifetime spent working farm fields with the rare old tractor.

The Rock Island Line

Dick Bockwoldt was brought up on a Rock Island tractor, so it isn't surprising he became one of the leading authorities on Rock Island tractor restorations. While Dick, who lives in Moline, Illinois, is a full-time old-tractor restorer, he readily admits he is not likely to get around to restoring all the tractors in his personal collection.

When he was interviewed for an article about his tractor collection by a reporter from a local newspaper, he summed things up this way: ". . . Just put some wrenches in my casket, and I'll keep working on them after I'm gone."

For Dick, as for so many other tractor collectors, word of mouth has been his most valuable tool in locating tractors. Being well known as a Rock Island tractor enthusiast and discussing Rock Islands whenever the opportunity arises led to one memorable find for him. Around 1987, a friend noticed an old Rock Island sitting in a yard on the other side of the Mississippi River near Muscatine, Iowa; of course, he told Dick about it right away.

At the time, Dick had three Rock Islands in his collection, but there was still room for more. So Dick called up his pal Kenny Lage, and the two of them hopped into Dick's pickup truck and made the trip across the river to see just exactly what kind of Rock Island was sitting there. They found what they were looking for on a small property that included a house and an old machine shop. The owner, now retired, worked only on occasional machining jobs and had no real use for the tractor.

After introducing themselves to the owner, the trio—Dick, Kenny, and the owner—walked over to the old Rock Island tractor and wound up giving it a thorough once-over. It was a 1929 Model F. As far as Dick was concerned, it was a gem of a find, even though it was badly in need of a restoration. After having seen all they needed to, they walked into the machine shop to get out of the cold winter weather.

Now the tricky part began. Dick wanted the tractor, but he didn't want to appear too eager. "I asked if it was for sale, and he said, 'Yeah it is; what will you give me for it?'" Dick said. The delicate dance continued as Dick repeatedly tried to get the elderly fellow to throw out a number. "I don't like to just make an offer. I prefer that they name a price," he said.

As the conversation continued, the owner asked what Dick planned to do with the tractor. When the fellow learned Dick was a Rock Island enthusiast who planned to restore it and add it to his collection, things seemed to take on a different tone. As Dick thinks back to the day, he suspects that if he had said he simply wanted to buy the tractor, restore, and resell it, things might have gone a different way.

Finally, after a bit of chin scratching and deliberation, the old fellow made a surprising offer. "I tell you what; you drink a cup of coffee with me, and I'll give it to you," he said. The deal caught both Dick and Kenny off guard.

Dick's response seemed a little surprising, too, at least to Kenny. "I don't drink coffee," Dick said.

"You mean you won't even drink a cup of coffee to get the tractor for nothing?" Kenny countered.

The situation seemed to take on the nature of a TV reality game show: do something disgusting to win a fabulous prize. Eventually, Dick swallowed hard and agreed to the "stunt" most people would have no problem with.

"I had to cut it fifty-fifty with milk. I still could hardly stomach it," Dick said.

A couple of days later, Dick returned with a trailer behind his pickup to load the tractor. The winter weather made loading the tractor a little difficult. The rubber tires were frozen into the mud and had to be pried loose before the Rock Island could be winched up onto the trailer. True to his word, the old gentleman helped load the F onto the trailer and waved goodbye without demanding a dime in payment.

"He just wanted someone to talk to for a while," Dick said of the old bachelor who let the old tractor go in exchange for a little company on a winter day.

All in all, the fellow made getting the F one of the most memorable experiences in Dick's tractor-collecting adventures, but he still shudders at the thought of having to down a cup of coffee, something he hasn't done since. "I'd rather have just bought it," he said.

Finding a Model G

A few years after the coffee adventure, Dick dug another F out of a mud bog and had just restored it when he received an interesting request. Representatives of the Dupont Company were planning to print a calendar featuring old farm tractors to promote the company's agricultural ventures, and they wanted to photograph one of Dick's Rock Islands to feature in it. Because the F was just finished, Dick offered it to them. The calendar featuring the F was distributed in several countries, and under the picture of the tractor was Dick's name and address along with a short narrative describing him as a Rock Island collector. Six years later, the appearance of that tractor in a calendar paid an unexpected dividend.

An antiques dealer in Manitoba had kept a copy of the now-outdated calendar, and he phoned Dick out of the blue with an interesting offer. "He said he knew where there was an old Rock Island and asked if I wanted it," Dick said.

Dick was interested and asked the caller to get him the serial number off the tractor so he could figure out exactly what it was. The next evening Dick's phone rang again, and the antiques dealer had discovered what kind of tractor he had found.

"When he said it was a Model G, my heart just about stopped," Dick said. He knew there were only two or three known examples of Model Gs in North America at the time. On top of that, the tractor's serial number showed it was only the fiftieth one made. "I didn't want to sound too enthusiastic, though." Dick said. "I asked how much he wanted, and he said fifteen-hundred U.S. dollars. I went to the bank the next day and had a cashier's check made out and sent it to him immediately."

Within a few days, Dick was on the road making the nine hundred–mile trek to get the tractor, which was on a farm a short distance outside the city of Winnipeg. When Dick arrived, the antiques dealer met him, and the two drove out to a farmyard where the G was sitting under a tarp. It was on steel wheels; remarkably, the engine wasn't stuck, and the magneto was still intact.

Apparently, the dealer had bought it from the farmer with the intent of finding a collector to resell it to. He had remembered seeing Dick's name on the old calendar and had actually called Dick the same day he bought the tractor. Clearly, he should have done a little research to find out exactly what he had before putting a price on it. A little while after bringing home his G, Dick saw one of the other few examples left sell for $53,000.

Once the G was in his workshop, Dick found that it was in remarkably good condition. It had a stuck valve and evidence of a repair to a crack in the engine. Luckily, the repair was still holding. The radiator also had a crack in it, but that kind of damage was small potatoes for Dick, who had a stock of Rock Island parts on hand that he acquired from swap meets and sales across the country.

Even though Dick may not get around to restoring all of the Rock Islands that stir memories of his youth, he's proved he'll go to great lengths to add yet another tractor to his collection—even if it means traveling nine hundred miles or drinking a cup of coffee.

Winning on a Long Shot

On his way out of a farmyard after attending an auction sale there, something caught Rene Vandoorne's eye—the hulk of an old tractor. It was hidden behind a grove of trees and almost completely obscured from any passersby. He hadn't noticed it before, and it wasn't included in the auction listing.

The next day, Rene called the farm owner and asked about the old tractor. He discovered that the recent auction sale on the property was organized by a woman selling off her farmer husband's belongings after he passed away. "I didn't think it was worth anything, so I didn't bother putting it in the sale," she told Rene when he asked about the tractor. So she didn't hesitate in agreeing to let Rene come out, take a closer look at the hulk, and possibly buy it for a parts tractor.

When he arrived back at the farmyard south of Brandon, Manitoba, Rene realized the old tractor was one of two that were hiding in the bush. There was a Cockshutt 30 nearby, as well. After coming to an agreement on price, Rene bought both tractors.

Nearly hidden by trees and almost unidentifiable, this Long Model A was missing an engine. The tractor's original owner decided it wasn't worth selling and left it out of an auction sale.

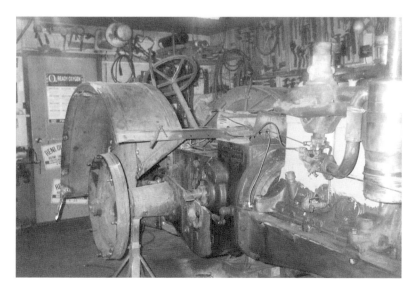

Shown here as it is about to get a new paint job, this 1935 Twin City tractor spent years inside a large shed. Only after the shed was removed could the tractor be seen from a nearby road.

"I didn't pay a lot, but I wasn't getting a lot, either," he said. That was certainly true. He wasn't even sure what the first tractor was. There were no decals remaining on the sheet metal anymore. "It was a real mess," he said.

At first, he thought the tractor was an old Farmall H or similar model because it had a raised section on the hood for a set of gauges and an exposed steering shaft.

On closer inspection, Rene found the tractor's serial number plate, and discovered it was a 1948 Long Model A. It certainly was a rare find in this area, or any other. What's more, like many other people, he had never even heard of Long tractors before meeting this old hulk in the trees.

After loading the two old machines and hauling them home, Rene parked them both in a shed on his property and let them sit for a while. His first thought was that both tractors would have no other use than to sacrifice themselves as parts donors. Neither one was complete, and both needed considerable effort to bring them back to life. He soon had a change of heart.

When he was looking through a book about old tractors he had recently bought, he found it had a listing for the estimated values for the two incomplete machines sitting in his shed. One of the listings caused him to do a double take; a restored Long, just like his, was worth about $9,000. That was significantly above the average price he could expect for the other more-common tractors in his collection. So Rene decided to take a second look at the Long and see what it would take to restore it.

His sons helped out with the research on the unfamiliar tractor by doing a little hunting on the internet; they were looking for anything they could find about the history of the tractor brand so Rene would have a starting point for the project. Their efforts paid off, and they were able to give their dad a wealth of information that would be vital in the restoration process.

The Long, Rene discovered, was built by a manufacturer that purchased most of the parts from other sources and bolted them together to create its own product. The entire transmission and rear-axle housing, complete with belt pulley, were bought from Cockshutt. That assembly was mated to a four-cylinder Continental engine.

Rene also found out that the Long Company started building tractors in 1948, the same year his Model A rolled off company lines. The A was only built for two years and then discontinued. Eventually, the company turned to importing tractors rather than continue building its own. With the original 162-cubic-inch Continental engine, Rene's Model A would have delivered 30 horsepower at the PTO.

After taking stock of the tractor in his shed, Rene realized that he had all the elements required to rebuild the Long, with the notable exception of the engine. It was clear the tractor had sat in its current condition, with the motor removed, for many years. The Long was then cast off to rust away in a grove of trees, exactly the spot Rene caught sight of it.

Seeing it there was a real stroke of luck for him—and the tractor. It likely would have remained there, becoming increasingly hidden by brush, if he hadn't seen it and been bold enough to call and ask about it. But now that he knew what it was, the trouble of getting it back to what it should be was ahead of him. Rene still needed a four-cylinder Continental engine to fill the void under the sheet metal.

Fortunately, a friend was restoring a tractor and had just removed the original Continental engine from it. "It was on a Twenty or a Twenty-Two Massey," Rene said. "He didn't think the engine was any good, so he pulled it out and put in a new one. I got the old one."

Rene put the engine in his shop and stripped it down. Luckily, it only needed to be cleaned up and have its valves redone. Another bargain for sure.

Once the engine was refurbished, Rene ran into another snag trying to put it in the Long. The left-side frame casting that ran along the engine was cracked. That may well have been the reason why the tractor was originally abandoned. Rene was not deterred. He welded the crack, restoring the frame's strength, and dropped the engine into place. When mated to the Cockshutt-built transmission, it was a perfect fit.

Once that was completed, the only other work the Long required was replacing a couple of bearings on the rear axle.

With the mechanical end of things finally addressed, now it was time to consider the cosmetics. Once again, Rene's luck held; a close inspection of the tinwork showed it was in remarkably good condition. There were no major dents or scratches. The only thing the Long really needed was a new coat of paint.

After the respray and applying a couple of decals that Rene was able to buy on the internet, the restoration was nearly complete. The tractor just needed some new shoes.

"When I found out the tractor could be worth nine thousand dollars, I thought it would be worth putting new tires on it," Rene said jokingly.

With new tires and a shiny suit of red paint, the Long Model A now looks as good as it did in 1948. What a remarkable transformation for a tractor whose previous owner didn't think it was worth selling.

Now that Rene had successfully rescued the Long and restored it to its former glory, he faced the challenge of refurbishing the Cockshutt 30. This tractor would be no easy fix, so he decided to let someone else take it on.

1935 Twin City FTA

Rene's Long-shot gamble on two old hulks paid off, but that wasn't the only time he rolled the dice and came up lucky on a tractor purchase. More than two decades ago, he caught a glimpse of another old machine looking forlorn in an abandoned homestead.

During a drive down a country road not too far from his farm, Rene noticed that the new owners of a farm had dismantled and removed a large storage shed that had stood there for years. In the process, the workers rolled an old tractor outside and out of the way so the shed could be moved to a new location.

Rene decided to take a closer look at the rusty old machine that was now sitting out in the elements. "At first I thought it was a 15-30," he said. Then he realized it was actually a 1935 Twin City FTA, and it was complete. Even more amazingly, it didn't look like anyone had the slightest interest in it. He instantly pictured the tractor becoming the newest addition to his collection.

First he had to find out who the owner was, so he drove to the neighboring farmyard and asked about the property. The neighbors told him that a Hutterite colony had just purchased the farmland from the previous owner, who was now retired. Coincidentally, Rene had a friend who knew the leader of that communal colony. So later in the week, after picking up his friend, Rene drove out to the colony to ask about the tractor.

"I decided I would go to five hundred dollars; so I took five one hundred–dollar bills with me," he said. The meeting went pretty well. The community all wanted to know about current events, he said, as the sect didn't allow its members to use any radios or televisions within the colony. When it finally came down to the negotiation, Rene offered $400 for the tractor. In the end, he and the colony's leader—or boss as he was referred to—struck a deal at $450.

"When I reached into my wallet to get the money and the boss saw the five one hundred dollar bills, he looked me square in the eye and said, 'You were going to pay five hundred, weren't you?'" Rene said. Rene conceded his observation was correct, but true to his word, the boss accepted $450 and Rene went to pick up the tractor.

After the Twin City was safely inside his workshop, Rene gave it complete inspection. The time it had spent hidden from the world, inside the now-dismantled shed, seemed to have spared it any serious harm from the elements. "I just cleaned it up and it ran," Rene said.

If only all tractor restoration efforts were that easy . . .

Firsts

Darold Sindt admits he has an obsession—his tractor collection includes about 400 machines, most vintage John Deeres. His collection is so impressive, in fact, that people at Deere and Company refer foreign visitors to him if they are interested in getting a good look at the history of North American farm tractors.

For Darold, one special tractor started it all: a 1937 John Deere Model A. It was included in the deal he struck to take over the John Deere dealership in Keystone, Iowa, from his former boss, Fred Schneider.

When Fred founded the Deere dealership in 1937, his father was his first customer, and the A was the first new tractor to roll out the door of the building. Fred's father owned the A until his death. Then the tractor sat in the old farmyard, unused, for more than a few years.

When Darold took over the dealership in 1968, Fred decided Darold should get the A along with the dealership. "He knew I always wanted to start a museum of old machinery," Darold said, and both knew the A was a great starting point.

Darold started working at the dealership right out of high school, in 1959. At the time, Fred said he would send Darold to the college of hard knocks as Darold learned his mechanic's trade. And that college was in Fred's back garage. In 1968, with his "college" education behind him, Darold was ready to run the business for himself.

As soon as the deal was finalized, Darold made the trip out to the farm where the A was sitting. "It hadn't been running for years," Darold said. "It was original and in real bad shape." So bad, in fact, that the engine's head had a hole in it, allowing water to penetrate inside.

The A was shod with factory-original steel wheels, making it one of the last As to be equipped that way. In 1938, most John Deere tractors coming off the assembly line had rubber tires.

With the first John Deere ever to be sold out of the Keystone dealership now safely stored away as a seed for a museum collection, Darold had a plan for one more addition to his collection. This one, however, would take years to develop. He wanted to get his hands on another first: the first tractor ever sold out of his own shop.

That tractor ended up being a 1967 Model 3020. Equipped with a gasoline engine, it was one of the last nondiesel versions. "Gas was still cheap back then, but diesel was even cheaper," Darold said. Despite that fact, future owner Harold Barron couldn't be talked out of his engine choice.

When Harold and Darold inked the deal on the tractor, Darold put his plan for the future in motion. There was a provision to the sale. Harold had to promise to trade the tractor back the next time he needed a new one. That way, the 3020 could eventually find its way into Darold's budding museum.

When the 3020 had logged 4,990 hours, Harold decided it was time to trade up. True to his word, he walked back into the dealership in 1982 and announced he had his eye on a new 4440 model. Once the two men agreed on a price, Harold once again took home a new tractor, and he left Darold's first new tractor sale on the dealership lot.

The 3020 wasn't retired from service, however. Despite being a valuable addition to the collection, Darold still puts the tractor through its paces, occasionally cutting grass with a three-point hitch mower.

That was a situation very different to what the A was capable of when it first came back to the lot. It wasn't running at all, and the day-to-day demands of operating his new business meant Darold didn't have much time to think about the A's restoration—at least right away. In fact, it wasn't until a local celebration was planned that Darold took steps to get the A up and running again.

When the small town of Keystone was about to celebrate its 100th anniversary, Darold wanted the A to march in the parade with more than 130 of his other antique tractors. So work got underway, and by 1981, the A was back in fine form. That year Darold also built a new building to house his business, and the old office and garage, which sat next door, became home to his museum.

Darold's family has since taken over the dealership, and Darold now claims to be retired. However, the demands of managing his collection and adding to the museum seem to be nearly a full-time job. Of course, if you love doing something as much as Darold loves working with his "obsession," is it really a job?

An Oliver with a Twist

When Bill Hogg of Swift Current, Saskatchewan, was looking for a hobby that he could share with his son, he decided to take up collecting toy tractors. The idea may have been spurred by the fact that Bill still had the toy tractor that came with the Oliver 77 his father bought new from a dealer in 1949, when Bill was a just boy.

Bill and his son eventually amassed a collection of toy tractors that numbered around 1,000 pieces. Then, after his son had grown, Bill decided to take a bold step forward and start collecting real tractors. His initial aim was to collect every model of Oliver tractor that his father had used on the family farm when Bill was growing up. Later he expanded his collecting to include all examples of that brand.

Over the years, Bill developed a keen eye for any potential addition to his full-sized tractor fleet. Eventually, a glimpse of a rare Oliver model set Bill on the longest negotiation of his life.

In early spring 2001, as near as Bill can remember, he was traveling down an unfamiliar highway with his grain truck and trailer to pick up a load of certified wheat seed for his farm. As he passed a small acreage near the town of Glidden, he noticed an unusual-looking Oliver sitting in the middle of the yard, which was about 100 yards off the road.

The tractor was a 1948 Model 88 with an uncommon, streamlined body style. "I knew it was rare," Bill said.

After loading his seed grain and heading back home, Bill couldn't resist the urge to get another look at the old machine. So as he approached Glidden for the second time, he brought his large truck to a stop on the side of the highway in front of the acreage where the tractor stood.

The tractor was still parked in the same spot, and Bill noticed it had a homemade dozer blade attached to it. It was clear that the tractor had been pushing snow recently.

Bill immediately knew he wanted to have the tractor for his collection, but he had no idea who lived in the small farmyard. "I don't like to interfere with anyone's privacy," he said, but the old Oliver was a real temptation. So Bill thought he would knock on the door unannounced and ask if the owner would sell it.

When Bill knocked on the door, an elderly couple appeared, and Bill got straight to the point. He introduced himself and asked about the tractor. The man said a lot of guys were interested in buying the tractor and he wasn't about to sell it. The couple still relied on the Oliver to keep the snow cleared from their yard during the winters. "That's the reason he didn't want to sell," Bill said.

More than a little disappointed, Bill handed the owner his business card and said he would be interested in buying it if the owner ever changed his mind. Then he walked back to his truck.

After six years of waiting, Bill Hogg now has this streamlined Oliver 88 in his workshop. It is in need of a complete engine overhaul and restoration. This extremely rare edition will likely become the centerpiece of Bill's all-Oliver tractor collection.

Bill couldn't forget the old Oliver, and he wasn't about to sit back and rely on luck to get him the tractor. After all, he had been told several people were just waiting to snap it up. He knew he would have to keep in touch with the couple and ensure that when they did decide to sell the tractor, he would have a chance to buy it.

"I phoned a couple of times a year. Just to touch base," Bill said. Finally, in spring 2007, the desire to have the Oliver in his collection was getting the better of him.

Finally, in spring 2007, the desire to have the Oliver in his collection was getting the better of him. He decided to just go ahead and tell the couple he really wanted the tractor and ask them to name their price.

He decided to just go ahead and tell the couple he really wanted the tractor and ask them to name their price. That is, of course, a risky request.

Undaunted, Bill placed a call to the couple around lunch time, and the woman answered. She said her husband wasn't in at the moment. "I asked if she remembered me, and she said yes. She told me they still had my card," Bill said. That was definitely a good sign. He spoke to her for a few minutes and then just came out with it the only way to say it: "Name your price." The woman paused a moment and then suggested he call back that evening, at supper time.

Bill made the second call as directed, and this time the man answered. Apparently, Bill's bold offer was one they just couldn't refuse; it finally convinced them after all those years that he really wanted to buy the tractor. "He named a price and I said okay," Bill said. Not wanting to wait too long and have the owners change their minds, Bill went to the bank the following morning to get a certified check to buy the tractor.

"We were in the middle of calving, and it wasn't the best time to go," Bill said, but he wasn't about to give up the once-in-a-lifetime chance to get the streamlined 88.

When Bill arrived at the farmyard to pick up the tractor, the elderly couple had already removed the dozer blade from the 88. The tractor was ready to load. "I was amazed they were able to do it," Bill said, noting how much difficulty the man had just walking around with his makeshift cane. "I tried to offer him some extra money for doing it, but the old fellow wouldn't take it. So I gave it to his wife and said at least take him out to dinner."

The old Oliver ran, but only barely. It was able to pull itself up onto the trailer and then into the workshop when Bill arrived back at his farm, but the engine was in dire need of a rebuild. The sheet metal, however, was straight and will be able to shine again without too much effort.

Checking the streamlined 88's serial number against AGCO's latest parts manual, Bill found out the tractor is one of only 485 built in 1947 and 1948. After that two-year production run, the streamlined model was discontinued. Yes, Bill had known it was rare, but not that rare!

"I'd like to show it next season," he said, which means he's going to have a busy fall and winter ahead of him.

CHAPTER FIVE

The Engagement Gift

The Engagement Gift

What do you get your fiancée for an engagement gift? Jewelry is probably the first thing that springs to mind, and an old tractor is likely the last—at least if you don't want her to break off the engagement and never speak to you again. Yet for Mary Kipp of Hillsboro, Ohio, a tractor was exactly what she wanted.

When Mary met her fiancé, Dave, he had been a tractor enthusiast and collector for some time. In his free time today, he often helps out his friend Bill Morris, who owns a tractor salvage yard in nearby Jamestown. Dave does some of the mechanical work to ready new arrivals to sell on Bill's lot.

On a summer day in 2000, Mary tagged along as Dave went to Bill Morris' salvage yard. His job that day was to change a tire on a 1942 narrow-front Farmall H that Bill was planning to offer for sale.

Bill had found the old H sitting in a barn in a local farmyard, and the elderly farmer hadn't used it in a very long time. In fact, the H had sat unused for ten or fifteen years before Bill pulled it out into the sunlight again. He brought it back to his lot and planned to get it fully functional once more; then he'd offer it for sale as a runner. It was definitely too good of a tractor to part out.

As Dave worked feverishly to win the bet he had made with Mary that he could change the rear tire in two hours using only hand tools, Mary sat and watched from nearby. As she studied the old H, she began to appreciate the styling that the International Harvester designers had given it. Naturally, she happened to mention to Dave that she liked the look of it. "I was sitting there passing tools and thinking this tractor was just the right size—not as big as Dave's M, but just big enough," she said.

Eventually, Dave and Mary took a brief pause from working as they waited for Bill to make a quick parts run to get something they needed for the tire repair. They decided to spend that free time giving the little H a closer inspection. As they continued to look over the tractor, they turned their attention to the engine. "Dave started it up, and I told him it sounded good," Mary said.

This Farmall H was Mary Kipp's engagement gift from her fiancé, Dave. At their outdoor wedding, Mary decided she wanted to drive the tractor "up the aisle" to the ceremony. Dave, too, arrived at the wheel of his own tractor.

After Mary first saw the Farmall at a local dealer, she mentioned she liked it. A few days later, Dave took Mary out to a friend's farmyard where he kept his own tractors. The Farmall H was there, waiting for her as a surprise gift.

Since meeting Dave, Mary had been to several tractor shows and events where Dave was displaying his Farmall M and F-20. Before meeting him, she really didn't know much about tractors. Now some of his enthusiasm for them was starting to rub off on her—maybe without her even realizing it.

After Bill returned with the needed parts, they went back to work on the tire-changing job. Not surprisingly, Dave won the bet by completing it within the allotted time. Yet Mary's observations and comments about the H didn't go unnoticed—Dave had an idea.

About a week later, Dave was at Mary's house visiting, and he said he had to make a quick phone call. After hanging up, he said, "We have to go out to Dale's house." Dale was a friend who allowed Dave to store tractors in his farmyard.

"There was nothing to suggest anything was different about this trip," Mary said. They often went out there to work on Dave's tractors or get them ready for upcoming shows.

When they arrived at Dale's, Dave said, "I have a surprise for you." As they walked to where the tractors were parked, she could see the H from Bill Morris' salvage yard parked beside Dave's M and F-20. "This is yours," he said, motioning to the H. "I bought it for you." Mary was taken completely by surprise.

A little while later, Dale came out to give them a little ribbing about parking another Farmall in his yard. He was an Oliver man, after all. Yet when he found out the new H was Mary's tractor, he told her it could stay, giving her a wink.

An informal, outdoor ceremony in which the Farmalls could take part was Mary's wish for her 2002 wedding. And that's exactly what she got. The tractors waited nearby as vows were exchanged.

Not too many women can say they threw their wedding bouquet from the driver's seat of a Farmall, but Mary can.

Although many men would expect to spend the next several days sending flowers to their fiancée and asking for forgiveness after giving a gift like that, Dave had nothing to fear. Mary was delighted with the H. Now she could participate in old-tractor events right alongside Dave with her very own Farmall. One that was, as she said, "just the right size."

When it eventually came time to finalize arrangements for their wedding in 2002, Mary was even more smitten with the old Farmalls. When she was asked what arrangements she would like for the ceremony, she said, "I want to include the tractors!" Clearly, having a wedding that would include the use of two Farmalls would have to be outdoors, and Dale generously offered the use of his farmyard for the event.

When the wedding day finally came, all of the couple's tractors had a part to play. The F-20 pulled a hay wagon that delivered guests from the parking area to the farmyard, where the reception and ceremony would be held. The M and the H would take center stage along with Mary and Dave.

The ceremony was held in front of a small pond, where the guests were gathered. The bride and groom approached at the same time, but from different sides. The bride, at the wheel of her very own Farmall H, drove straight up to the pond in front of the guests, just as any bride would come up the aisle. Dave, on the other hand, approached from behind the pond on the M and parked it in front of Mary and the H. Then the bride and groom dismounted, and the ceremony began.

After the "I dos," the bride and groom got back on their tractors. This time they drove away, side by side. After driving out of sight, they both returned with their tractors for the reception.

Keeping with the unique flair of their wedding, Dave and Mary decided their wedding reception would be a wiener roast where all the young kids in the crowd could have a chance to have a ride on the tractor of their choice.

Since the wedding, there's been an addition to Dave and Mary's family. No, not the kind of addition you're likely thinking of: It's another Farmall. This time another F-20. There was no word, though, on whether Dave was handing out cigars when it joined the family.

CHAPTER SIX

Around the World

Island Hopping

Although hundreds of Farmall tractors were put to work in the row-crop regions of New Zealand's North Island, only a few McCormick W-6 models—another tractor made under the International Harvester Corporation's umbrella—could be found here.

David Hogan, a New Zealand tractor restorer and International Harvester enthusiast, estimates that only about six examples of the W-6 were ever in the whole eastern region near Poverty Bay. The bay was named by famed explorer Captain James Cook, but it hardly does justice to the region, which is one of the most fertile places in the world.

When the International Harvester W-6 arrived at the Hogan's home, it was still covered in a layer of dust and bird droppings. The burlap over the exhaust pipe was to prevent sea water from getting into the engine during the ferry crossing to New Zealand's North Island.

Many of the W-Series International tractors had been imported to the island country to do land-clearing work, which they excelled at. Equipped with steel wheels and fitted with heavy, angle-iron bumpers, these solid tractors pushed through scrub and brush, knocking it down and pulling heavy disks to till up the ground. They performed the work usually reserved for crawlers, but David believes they did their job much more cheaply.

The fact that so few of these tractors were ever sold in this part of New Zealand made the W-6 a sought-after tractor for any local hard-core IH collector, such as David and his wife, Janet, who now live near the city of Hastings. However, that wasn't the main reason the Hogans wanted to add a W-6 to their ever-growing family of Internationals.

Janet's grandfather had farmed eighty acres of land in the Poverty Bay region, and he had owned one of the few W-6s to ever reach this area. So with fond memories of

After only three months in David and Janet Hogan's workshop, the W-6 was ready for showing. The headlights on the W-6s imported into New Zealand are positioned lower than those on North American models.

Granddad's W-6 and the appeal of this rare model, David and Janet could not squelch their desire to park one of these tractors in the midst of their collection.

David and Janet hadn't been able to find one for sale locally, despite the connections they had made by being members of the Hawke's Bay Vintage Machinery Collector's Club. After deciding the time was right to start looking for a W-6, they placed an ad in *The New Zealand Farmer's Weekly*, one of New Zealand's national newspapers. They soon received five responses. However, after checking the tractors out, it was apparent that they were all nearly reduced to the status of parts donors. Restoring any of them would be a costly and time-consuming adventure. Just as things were looking a little bleak for the prospects of finding a W-6, the sixth response showed a lot more promise. The only catch with this one was that the owner wouldn't let just anyone buy the tractor.

The eighty-year-old owner of this particular W-6 had purchased it new in 1948. He had proudly driven it the ninety miles from the dealership to his farm at Mayfield, Canterbury, on New Zealand's South Island, where it had been ever since. For the last forty years, the W-6 had been parked, unused, inside a stable, relatively safe from the elements. When the owner spotted the Hogans' ad, he had his son call and check them out.

Yes, he was ready to part with the W-6, but it had to go to a proper home, a place where it would be restored to its former glory and definitely not scavenged for parts. Proving that they were worthy of buying the W-6 was the first step for the Hogans in the negotiation process. "When he realized that we were genuine vintage-tractor buffs, he couldn't do enough for us," David said.

Still, David had to negotiate a price. Because of the distance involved, all negotiations took place over the phone. Neither the Hogans nor the owner and his son had actually met, and they both had to operate on trust. David and Janet were trusting the owner's description of the tractor and its history, while the owner and his son were trusting David and Janet really would take care of this prized machine. After three days of back-and-forth negotiating, a deal was struck. Now, David's next task was arranging to get the W-6 home.

Finding someone to haul the W-6 for the twelve-hour trip from the owner's stable to the Hogans' home—plus six hours on a ferryboat during the crossing from the South Island to the North Island—would not be a problem. Getting it done at an affordable cost would.

"It took about a fortnight to get here," David said of the W-6's trip. "They had to fit in other freight around it." Including the W-6 with other partial freight shipments reduced the transportation cost significantly.

When the W-6 arrived at the Hogans' home, they weren't disappointed. Aside from having a covering of years of stable dust and enough bird droppings to almost convince someone that a can of white paint had been spilled over it, the W-6 was in excellent condition. Incredibly, it still had its original tires and exhaust pipe.

The tractor was also equipped with a front-mounted sickle-bar sharpening attachment. Run off the belt pulley, this sharpener was used to sharpen mower and combine cutter bars. That may have been useful in its day, but David and Janet quickly removed it.

After three months in the Hogans' workshop, the tractor looked like new again. Nothing more than cosmetic work was required to make the W-6 the pride of the Hogans' collection.

To prove they had stayed true to their word and restored the W-6, David and Janet sent the original owner a photo of the refurbished tractor. "He couldn't help but shed a tear as he said it was just the way he bought it in 1948," David said. "But there was something missing—it was the rear wheel weights that I had taken off. The old chappie missed nothing."

1955 Farmall Super FC-C

Mentioning that she would really like to add a Farmall H to their vintage-tractor collection seemed like just polite small talk for Janet when she and David were dining with friends in Waipukurau. Unexpectedly, their host casually replied that one such tractor had been parked on a nearby hillside for at least the past six years.

The news was like a bolt from the blue. David and Janet could end their search for the next tractor for their collection, and both were eager to see this long-forgotten machine. When their host suggested they drive right over and check it out, the group of friends was on the road in no time.

As they drove down the road amid the rolling countryside, they could see the tractor appear off in the distance. "Janet said to me, 'That doesn't look like an H,'" David said. As they pulled off the road in front of a grassy paddock, it was clear that this indeed wasn't an H. But it was a Farmall, and it looked complete. In fact, it still had a bean cultivator attached to it.

The tractor was a 1955 French-made Farmall FC-C row-crop model, and it had been in this spot for so long it seemed to have taken root, literally. All four tires had sunk into the earth up to the rims, making it look as if it had sprouted and grown there. A cursory inspection showed that the engine was seized, but apart from that, the tractor looked okay.

"We didn't really want a French tractor, but we could see the potential in this one," David said. It wasn't an H, but it would make a fine addition to their IH collection, nonetheless. Now they had to figure out who owned it.

The group stopped at a neighboring farmyard and asked the farmer about the property and the old tractor.

While looking for a Farmall Model H, the Hogans were directed to this
tractor, which had been sitting unused in a paddock for about six years.
The tractor turned out to be a French-made Farmall Model FC-C.

The owner, they found out, lived in Hastings, the same city
Janet and David were currently living in.

"It took about a week to find the owner, and he was so
reluctant to sell," David said. "The negotiation process was
a bit like 'yes I will, no I won't.' I had to be very diplomatic
and convince him." If something wasn't done before too
much more time went by, the tractor could deteriorate
beyond repair. David and Janet left the owner with that
thought and went home, hoping to hear from him again.

The acreage where the FC-C sat slowly fading away
was owned by an engineer who had intentions of someday
building a house and starting his own vegetable farm. That
dream had not yet materialized, and for all intents and
purposes, it likely wouldn't any time soon.

A week later, David and Janet's phone rang. The
engineer had decided he wanted to make a deal after all.

Despite a seized engine, the FC-C cleaned up nicely after some mechanical and cosmetic work. Here, it's on display at a vintage-machinery show attached to an IHC B46 hay baler.

"We went around and paid for it that evening," David said. Both the engineer and his wife were concerned that their little tractor end up in good hands, despite their seeming abandonment of it. "When he realized we were vintage-machinery buffs and enjoyed restoration, he was much easier about it," David said.

French-made tractors were imported into New Zealand in modest numbers during the 1950s, due to a government policy that tended to favor British Commonwealth imports or other European imports. Nowadays, finding similar examples of these tractors in New Zealand is not easy. The question, though, is if the Hogans' collection of old Internationals has been filled to capacity. No, it's still growing. It seems the couple likes to get their hands dirty breathing new life into old, red machines. If there's a vintage International tractor hiding anywhere on New Zealand's islands, the Hogans will likely find it—sooner or later.

A Case of
La Dolce Vita

For twenty-four-year-old Davide Lorenzone, old tractors, engines, and steamers have always held a special fascination. And it's probably fair to say that this civil-engineering student, who now spends most of his time studying at the university in Turin, Italy, is one of a very few students who has his own vintage tractor at home.

Davide's tractor is a 1938 Case Model R, which now makes its home in Albugnano, in northwestern Italy—Davide's hometown. The R is, no doubt, as unique in that town as an old-tractor fan such as Davide is at Turin's university—especially, considering the R was originally sold new and spent all of its working life in Argentina.

Davide spent about five years living in Buenos Aires, until he and his family moved back to Italy in 2000. During that time, Davide traveled extensively around Argentina, and he often got to see old tractors taking part in parades and expositions in many of the rural towns in the countryside. It was a real treat for the budding engineer. Although he wanted to have one of those grand old machines for himself, that would have to wait.

On a holiday to South America in 2003, Davide Lorenzone found this 1938 Case Model R, which had been sitting under a eucalyptus tree in Argentina since 1960. When Davide first saw it, the retired owner happened to be sitting nearby and gave him a full history of the tractor.

In February 2003, Davide crossed the Atlantic Ocean again; this time he and a friend, who had a passion for old tractor collecting, went to visit Davide's old school chums and spend time in the country he had called home for so long. When Davide and his friends were back together again, they did what all young men would do: They went on a road trip. Fortunately, Davide had at least one Argentine friend who shared his passion for old iron, so checking out the tractor sights as they traveled was high on their list of priorities.

Davide's pal from Argentina mentioned seeing a small rusty and dirty old tractor sitting in a grove of trees near the town of Concordia, in the province of Entre Rios. The tractor had been sitting there as long as the friend could remember, and Davide knew he had to take a look at it.

When they arrived at the old tractor, Davide found it just as his friend had described it. It was rusty and dirty, and it was sitting partly hidden by tall grass under a very large eucalyptus tree. Not far away was an elderly man about eighty-five years old sitting and watching the young men inspect the tractor. He turned out to be the owner of the farm and the tractor. Davide convinced the old man to tell him about the tractor's history.

What followed was an entertaining tale, as the old farmer reminisced about how his father had bought the tractor new and used it to pump water for the farm's cattle and plough the fields. His memories were liberally peppered with interesting anecdotes.

The tractor had been in regular use up until 1960, the owner said, when it eventually was no longer useful. It had been parked under the eucalyptus tree the last time it was used. No doubt with younger members of the family tending to most chores on the farm these days, it seemed as if the farmer himself had been put out to retirement under his own eucalyptus tree, with the tractor for company.

On closer inspection, there really didn't seem to be anything wrong with the old Case or any reason for it to have been abandoned, other than the obvious fact there were now newer and more modern machines to do its job. As far as Davide could tell, the sheet metal was in good shape, and a twist of the crank showed the engine spun freely with a reasonable amount of compression in the cylinders.

Captivated by the tractor and the tales of its exploits around the Argentine farm, Davide had to have the tractor. "When I saw it, I said, 'Yes, this is the tractor that I want!' It was small and nice, but I decided to buy it because I met the first owner and talked with him about the story of the tractor," Davide said.

So Davide made a deal for the tractor on the spot and began making arrangements to get it back to Italy. Davide's traveling companion had already found two tractors he had to have and purchased them, so they split the cost of a shipping container and arranged to have the tractors loaded for the voyage home. Five weeks later, the container was offloaded at the Savona seaport and delivered to Davide's friend's home.

After getting the R home, Davide thoroughly inspected the tractor and began the process of getting it running again. Starting with the basics, he changed the electrical cables running from the magneto and cleaned out the fuel tank, among other things. Then, deciding to put the Case's engine to the test, Davide walked to the front of the tractor and gripped the crank. After two spins, the tractor fired and ran as if it had been parked for a few days instead of a few decades.

Davide had only managed to put a few miles on the tractor driving through the Italian countryside when the old R started to spit out oil and make some strange and unsettling sounds. The strain of the recent use had been too much for some old bearings and gaskets, which now needed replacement. Getting parts for the R in Europe proved to be a real challenge, however.

After putting the R project on hold for a while due to his studies, Davide returned to it in 2005 and began searching in earnest for parts and a shop manual to help with the needed restoration. Davide found what so many other tractor collectors have: The internet is a saving grace in finding the impossible. He was able to source the parts and manuals he needed in the United States.

After crossing the Atlantic in a shipping container, the old Case looks right at home in Albugnano, Italy. Although it has been fully restored now, the tractor did start right up after Davide bought it, and it ran for several months after only some minor attention.

Today, the R is completely restored and looks like the pride of Italy, but Davide isn't content to leave things there. He is now trying to track the tractor's history from the time it left J. I. Case's assembly plant to its appearance on the farm in Argentina. If the past performance of this industrious student is any indicator, he'll soon know.

Radio Recovery

Lincolnshire, in England's East Midlands, is a rural county, with much of the population living and working on farms. So perhaps it isn't too surprising that Barbara Stimpson, a broadcast journalist with BBC's Radio Lincolnshire, sooner or later would find herself closely linked to a farm tractor.

In 2000, the BBC launched a program, *The Search*. "It offered a chance to find special people and cherished possessions, which had gone missing from people's lives," Barbara said. Basically, the radio station offered assistance to any of its listeners who were searching for something, and Barbara was one of the people responsible for doing the legwork.

When the Lincolnshire radio station announced the program over the air, Mike Waterhouse was listening in from the cab of his tractor as he worked a field on his farm in neighboring Nottinghamshire. It sounded like the perfect solution to his problem. "I'd been thinking about the IH 634 tractor we had new on the farm in 1970 and used for five years before trading it. I always said I would like to find it again, if it had not been scrapped," he said.

If he had waited a little longer to ask for
help in finding the tractor, it would likely
have already gone to a new owner,
making the search that much more
difficult—and maybe even impossible. . . .

When it was new, the tractor hadn't gone far from the
Doncaster factory where it was built before Mike bought it.
P. Platts and Sons, an IH dealer, had it on its lot, which was
just a little way down Wheatley Hall Road from IH's plant.

So as soon as he heard about the program, Mike
immediately called the radio station on his cell phone—
right from the tractor. Maybe they could find the 634 for
him, he thought.

Barbara Stimpson took the call and listened to Mike
describe the tractor he was looking for. "It's fair to say
the tractor search was one of the most unusual ones we
had," Barbara said. Fortunately, she had a valuable aid in
the search. The old 634, like all farm tractors in the United
Kingdom, had a registration number that was displayed
like a license plate, and Mike could still remember that
number: EDT 363J. He also knew that a farmer named
Bradshaw had purchased the tractor from the dealership
after Mike had traded it in on a 7000 Ford back in 1975.

In an effort to involve the station's listeners in the
search, the quest for Mike's old tractor was announced over
the air, and anyone with information was encouraged to call
in. "We broadcast the appeal several times," Barbara said,

and that approach eventually paid off. "We got a response a few weeks later from someone who knew the Bradshaws."

A member of the Bradshaw family still owned the tractor, so Barbara was heading in the right direction. That original tip eventually led her to a farm in Lincolnshire that wasn't too far from Mike's, and that's where the old tractor was. After following up and confirming the registration number, Barbara was ready to call Mike and give him the good news. She had also discovered that the current owner was willing to sell the 634, which would be the icing on the cake for Mike.

"For three or four weeks I didn't hear anything," Mike said. Then he got the call from Barbara. He was pretty happy, to say the least. About a week later, Mike was standing in a field where the 634 with registration number EDT 363J was parked with some other implements.

The tractor's current owner had planned on selling the farm and all the equipment. So to get things ready for sale, all the machinery had been moved into the open field across the road from the farm buildings. That way, the house and yard could be sold.

The timing couldn't have been better for Mike. If he had waited a little longer to ask for help in finding the tractor, it would likely have already gone to a new owner, making the search that much more difficult—and maybe even impossible—for Barbara.

By now, the 634 was only a shadow of the tractor it used to be. "I hadn't seen it in twenty-five years," Mike said, and he was in for a bit of a shock. It now had a front-end loader attached to it, and it had seen quite a few years of hard graft since Mike had owned it. It didn't even run anymore. The clutch was worn out and, aside from looking more than a little worse for wear, it need a thorough restoration.

However, it was the tractor Mike had dreamed of finding, so he asked if he could buy it. After offering the owner a check for what Mike estimated to be its worth, "he pretty near snapped my hand off," Mike said. There was no question that the owner was willing to take whatever he could get for the dilapidated tractor in order to rid himself of it.

Mike is now pleased to report that the tractor is back in his shed "being done up." This means that before too much more time has passed, the 634 will look as good as it did the day it first arrived on Mike's farm in 1970. And the BBC's Radio Lincolnshire now has one very loyal listener by the name of Mike Waterhouse.

For the Father
Who Has Everything

Most tractor collectors and enthusiasts imagine themselves on the buying end of a tractor deal rather than on the selling end. I guess acquiring a new machine more easily evokes the imagination and excitement than selling one off does. However, for Paul Lakeman, it was selling a classic that sticks in his mind as one of the more memorable moments in his collecting experience, and he's bought and sold more than a few old tractors.

Paul has his home and workshop on an acreage along the busy Trans-Canada Highway near the city of Regina, Saskatchewan. More than a few of the machines in his collection of vintage tractors and machinery can be seen sitting in his yard by passing motorists.

"I get a lot of people stopping in here and wanting to talk about old tractors," Paul said. And that should be no surprise to anyone who has seen his impressive collection. Paul has had literally hundreds of old tractors pass through his hands. "I usually get them at auction sales," he said.

On one occasion, Paul remembers attending a vintage-tractor sale in British Columbia—about nine hundred miles from his home—with another collector friend from the Regina area, and between the two of them, they bought most of the tractors in the sale. "We went a little crazy," he said. It took a couple of semi-trailer trucks to haul all the old tractors home.

It was one of those auction-sale tractors that Paul had sitting in his front yard that attracted the attention of a passing truck driver. One afternoon a few years ago, Paul noticed a semi-trailer truck stopped on the highway in front of his home and the driver walking into his yard.

The driver had noticed Paul's restored 1946 Farmall M and wanted to have a closer look at it. The driver had seen it sitting there some time ago, and every time he went by, he'd look for it. Finally, he decided to stop in.

The two men talked for a little while, and Paul found out that the driver had originally grown up on a farm in Brazil. The driver's father was one of the first farmers in that particular district of Brazil to own an M. Seeing Paul's M sitting alongside the highway made the driver think of his father's tractor.

At the end of their conversation, the driver asked Paul how much it would take to buy the M, but Paul wasn't in the mood to sell it. So the M stayed put. Over the course of the next six months, the driver occasionally came back for yet another look at the tractor, and each time the topic of conversation would turn to selling. However, Paul continued to turn down the driver's offers to purchase it. Eventually, Paul relented, and the two struck a bargain.

The truck driver told Paul he now lived in Winnipeg, Manitoba, but the tractor wouldn't be going there. The tractor was going to be loaded into a shipping container for a much longer trip; it was heading to Brazil. It was going to be a gift for his father, who was now retired.

After negotiating the purchase of the tractor, the driver contacted a museum in the region of Brazil where his father had farmed, and it was interested in acquiring the M, too. So an agreement was reached that would see the M put on display in the museum for a specified time; in return, the museum would cover the shipping costs necessary to get the old tractor to South America. The driver's father would have to make the trip to the museum to see his new, old M, at least for the first year or two. On schedule, the truck driver arrived in Paul's yard with a container trailer to load the M, and a neighbor came over to lend Paul and the truck driver a hand. That was the last Paul saw of the M or the driver, and he never did hear how the tractor has since fared. But as a proud father himself, Paul was pleased to have been associated with the old M that set sail for South America to become another father's special gift.

Hard to Part With

Ask vintage-tractor dealer Urs Eberhart what stands out in his mind as the most memorable moment during his time buying and selling old iron, and the answer is a little unexpected. It isn't really any one particular hunt, he said, but the people he meets. "I've had some guys who seem to have a very hard time selling," he added. Their emotional attachment to their old tractors makes parting with them difficult, even when they want to make a sale.

One particular person stands out in Urs' mind when he talks about the people he's met locating old tractors in Western Canada and the Northwestern United States for export to Europe. This seller owned two John Deere Model As and really had a hard time letting them go.

Bill, the seller, was an elderly man, and Urs went to the town of Eckville, Alberta, to meet him and see the tractors he had for sale. Bill said he had been working on restoring the two Model As for four or five years. Now he wanted to sell them because his health was failing.

Finding the two As was routine enough at the start; Urs simply responded to an ad in a local newspaper. During an initial phone call, Bill and Urs discussed the two Deeres.

About two weeks after that first contact, Urs made the forty-five-minute trip from his home in Olds to the acreage where Bill lived and had the two tractors stored.

"Some guys don't want to sell to me if the tractors are going overseas," Urs said, but Bill didn't seem to have any trouble with that notion. Though, it was plain to see he was passionate about the two old Johnny Poppers.

Bill had owned a John Deere dealership throughout his life. So his fondness for the tractors was not only that he had restored them, but also that he could probably remember selling tractors just like them from his own shop—or possibly even these very same ones.

After spending some time with Bill and the two old Deeres, Urs left for home and began putting together a deal with his connections in Switzerland, his native country. About four or five weeks later, everything was arranged, and Urs returned to Bill's to pick up the tractors.

"He wanted to sell them, but when it came to the sale—when the tractors actually left his yard—he had a hard time with it," Urs said. It was plain that if Bill was healthier, younger, or both, he wouldn't have parted with them for anything.

"He had mixed feelings; he was glad they were going to a good home. He was happy the tractors were gone, but he was sad to see them go. He was losing some of his history," Urs said.

A short time later, the two As, along with two other John Deeres—a D and an LA—acquired from other deals, were loaded into a shipping container in Urs' yard and sent off on their trip across the Atlantic to Switzerland. One A went into the collection of a noted enthusiast, while the other went to a young fellow who had few, if any, tractors in his stable.

Perhaps Urs was right about his conclusion that Bill was losing some of his history. However, he took comfort in the thought that Bill would have his memories of those tractors for the rest of his life. And when that young collector in Switzerland, who bought one of the tractors, reaches old age and his health is failing, how will he view the old A that joined his collection near the beginning? Will it bring back thoughts of a happy time? Will the tractors have been integral to many of his family's experiences as the years passed?

Just like the day Urs met with Bill and listened to him talk about the two tractors, will the day the A is next sold be one of mixed emotions? Will another thoughtful buyer take the time to listen to that fellow's recollections about the day the tractor was backed out of a shipping container, after a long voyage from Canada? I hope so.

CHAPTER SEVEN

Finding the Parts

Every once in a while, tractor enthusiasts discover that adding a rare old model to their collection is the easy part. Actually getting together enough of the proper parts to make that machine run again is where the difficulty really begins. And that's particularly true for many of the "orphan" brands: those tractors whose marquees have fallen into obscurity as a result of the rise and fall of corporations.

Sometimes, it's just the rarity of the parts you need that makes the hunt for them a real challenge. The possibility that just the right part, in factory fresh condition, is lying under a pile of rusty sheet metal in some nearby barn keeps restorers actively hunting, despite the odds.

As it turns out, collectors are frequently successful in finding those rare parts, and more often than you'd think. This chapter shares some of those stories.

A Tap on the Shoulder

Wouldn't it be nice if someone would just come up, tap you on the shoulder, and say, "I have the parts you need to restore that tractor"? But get real. That isn't likely to happen, is it? If you ask Rene Vandoorne, he would say it could, because it did happen to him.

Rene noticed an Oliver HG crawler on the sale bill for a farm auction near Franklin, Manitoba, and he decided it would make a great addition to his collection. So he showed up on sale day to have a look at it and maybe bring it home.

As is usual at a farm sale, the smaller items sell first. While checking them out, Rene noticed a seat that would fit a Minneapolis-Moline U, and it just so happened that the U in his own collection was missing that particular item. Of course, the Minneapolis seat was tied to another one, and the pair would sell together. Rene didn't know what the other seat was from. Yet when they went on the block, the price was right, so he bid and bought them both. Of course, he would have rather the auctioneer sold them separately.

After that, Rene went to have another look at the Oliver HG. As he inspected the little crawler, it didn't look too bad.

It did have one serious flaw, though. The auction company gave everyone special notice that the crawler's engine was stuck, and the tractor wouldn't start or run. Since there was no reason to believe there was anything else wrong with it, aside from missing a seat, Rene decided to bid on it. Hopefully, he could get it for a reasonable price.

The auctioneer made his way around to the crawler in due course, and Rene was the one to place the last, winning bid. The price he had to pay wasn't too bad, so he was excited about his new purchase.

With more machinery left to sell, the auctioneer and most of the crowd continued to move along as the sale went on, but Rene stayed behind to give his newest purchase another close inspection. A couple of other interested people also stayed to look over the crawler and chat; one of them, a complete stranger, had some unsettling news for Rene.

"He said they had it running before the sale started, and it stopped with a big clunk that popped the air breather off," Rene said. After that, the tractor wouldn't start, and the crankshaft wouldn't turn, the fellow explained. "I thought, oh no . . . I just bought the thing. That wasn't what I wanted to hear," Rene said.

Expecting that the engine had just seized up from sitting, like so many do, Rene was taken aback to find the Oliver had a serious mechanical problem. He knew from the man's description of what had happened that the engine had likely thrown a rod. Getting it running again would involve more than just freeing some stuck pistons. With damage like that, it might not even be possible to repair the engine.

Thankfully, the stranger, who was the bearer of bad news, wasn't the only person to speak up. Having overheard the conversation about the motor, another fellow came up to Rene and told him, "I've got an engine that'll fit in that cat." That news was music to his ears and quite an unbelievable circumstance. But it was true. The bystander's name was Fred Howard, and he was kind of a wheeler and dealer in the tractor world. Fred bought and sold a lot of vintage farm equipment and lived only a short trip away, in a town called Newdale.

With an unbelievable stroke of luck, Rene had finished his parts hunting before he even walked over to pay the auction company for his new purchase. "I've been lucky with mechanical things like that," he said.

With his mind a little more at ease now that the engine trouble was addressed, Rene turned his attention back to his newly acquired Oliver. As he looked at the seat mounting bracket, a light bulb went on in his head. He picked up the spare seat that came attached to his purchase for the U and set it in place. Not only did it fit, but it was clear that this was the seat that had been removed. Even the color matched. It's hard to say what reason someone would have had for taking it off in the first place.

Rene's luck was certainly holding true that day. If he hadn't needed a seat for his U, he wouldn't have paid any attention to the green metal one that was attached to it.

After getting the Oliver home, Rene put it into his workshop and stripped down the original engine. As he suspected, one of the connecting rods had snapped, and that's why the crankshaft wouldn't turn. He didn't have to

After buying this Oliver HG crawler at an auction, Rene Vandoorne had found all the necessary parts to get it up and running before he had even paid the auction company's cashier. A bystander offered to sell him a replacement engine on the spot.

try and find any replacement parts, though, because he'd already made the trip to Fred Howard's and picked up the four-cylinder replacement engine.

Once that replacement was installed, the crawler fired to life. Driving it around, Rene was pleased that the little machine was now in fine working order. And with his spare seat properly attached in its rightful place, Rene could even sit down to drive it.

Digging Up Skeletons

Don McKinley has a passion for old iron. However, his collecting started off a little differently than that of most other vintage-tractor enthusiasts.

When he was at a restored tractor show, he overheard a conversation between a boy and his father. The boy, who had been looking curiously at the display, turned to his father and said, "What did they use them for, Dad?"

"They farmed with them," the father said curtly. The more Don thought about what he had overheard, the more he realized that tractors had taken center stage in the collector world, while the implements they powered or pulled had been virtually forgotten.

To address that inequality, Don decided that he would gather together a full line of equipment that a farmer in the 1930s would, or could, have had. Then he would open a museum and allow fathers to bring in their sons and definitively answer the "What did they use them for?" question. Don's museum opened in 1993, but before it did, he knew he needed to have at least one display tractor, despite the museum's emphasis on implements.

The decision as to what tractor to include in the display was an easy one. Don's older brother had owned a John Deere Model B many years ago when he farmed near Quincy, Iowa, and Don had often been given the chance to drive it. Having a B in the collection would be like having an old friend help with the museum project. The B was a relatively popular tractor, and restorations on old Deeres are relatively easy, given the availability of new, original-equipment parts. So finding one wasn't too hard.

Marvin Huber, Don's son-in-law, who had several useful contacts through his job at the local John Deere dealer, made a couple of phone calls on Don's behalf and tracked down a restored B from an Iowa collector.

As far as Don was concerned, that was only half the job. Don's brother's B had been shod with skeleton steel wheels—so named because of their bare-bones look—and the B Marvin found had rubber tires. It just wasn't close enough to Don's recollections of his brother's old tractor. So the hunt began for a full set of skeleton steel wheels.

"I spent about two-hundred-plus dollars on phone bills," Don said about his efforts to track down the skeleton wheels. "I called all over the United States and Canada trying to find them." Nothing suitable turned up.

At about that time, the John Deere dealership where Marvin worked underwent an expansion, and after settling into his just-renovated office, Marvin moved in a scale model of an old Deere tractor with steel wheels and placed it on a shelf for display. The building contractor happened to walk in to check out the carpentry work in the office when he noticed the model tractor.

"I have an old tractor like that," he said, "but I replaced those steel wheels with rubber tires." That comment definitely caught Marvin's attention.

"What did you do with the steel wheels?" he asked.

"Oh, they're lying around behind the shed," he replied. When Marvin asked if he would sell them, the builder seemed happy just to get rid of them.

Marvin and Don drove over right away for a look. Just as he claimed, the builder had a full set of four skeleton steel wheels lying in the grass. They were exactly what Don was looking for. Yes, despite following up leads that had him calling all over North America, the wheels he needed were only three and a half miles from his home in Quincy. A deal was quickly made, and Marvin and Don loaded up all four skeletons and hauled them back to Don's.

The rear wheels were in good shape, but their bolt-on lugs needed to be replaced. The front wheels weren't perfect either. They needed some serious rebuilding, so they were sent out to a local machine shop for the needed restoration. Finding lugs for the rears meant that, once again, Don was on the phone in search of replacements—again, without any luck.

Aside from trying to get the parts to make the B look just the way he wanted it to, Don was also busy tracking down implements for the museum. He managed to find an old cultivator that he wanted at a local wrecking yard.

When he and Marvin went to load it and bring it home, Don casually asked the owner if he had any steel-wheel parts. "No," the fellow said, "But I might know who does." The owner then disappeared inside and made a phone call to a friend. He came back out a few minutes later and gave Don and Marvin directions to follow that took them about three miles down the road to the home of another old-machinery enthusiast.

When Don and Marvin arrived, they were shown into a workshop. Inside, the owner reached under a workbench and pulled out a loop of cable that held two brand-new full sets of wheel lugs. Incredibly, the original shipping tag from the John Deere works where they were manufactured was still attached.

Fortunately for Don, this enthusiast bought out the parts stock of a John Deere dealer that was going out of business many years ago. The lugs were part of the inventory the dealer had that had never been sold. With that stroke of luck, Don had found new, factory-original replacement lugs for his wheels. Unbelievable. And for the second time, the parts he needed were virtually in his own backyard.

Don's B now looks just like his brother's did, and the tractor, complete with skeleton steel wheels, plays center stage in Don's implement museum in Quincy.

One Piece at a Time

For those few who long to get into the steam traction engine hobby, finding complete engines, it seems, has been a tall order. That's why so many have turned to collecting steam engine parts, with the hope of eventually getting together enough of the right ones to assemble them into a complete, functioning machine.

And, as it turns out, finding the parts is no easy task either. For Bob Anderson of MacGregor, Manitoba, constructing his 25-75 Garr-Scott piece by piece was probably a more difficult task than most. So difficult, in fact, that by the time the tractor was built, he was able to write an article about his adventures for *Engineers and Engines* magazine.

Back in 1978, Bob decided he wanted to take a plunge into the world of steam tractors. He was raised on a prairie farm and still farms today. So he had been around steamers and, like any farmer, he was well aware of the important role they played in opening up the North American heartland to farming. What more reason do you need to be interested in these venerable old machines?

As Bob was about to discover, however, he would need patience, determination, and, maybe above all, a good balance in his checking account to truly get into this hobby. Eventually, his parts hunting led him across five Canadian provinces and seven U.S. states in search of enough of the right components to piece together his Garr-Scott.

"I was really looking for a Waterloo, the make I'd grown up on, so to speak," Bob said. But there were none to be found. Eventually, Jack Beamish, another steam enthusiast, convinced Bob to build his own tractor. "I know where there's a Garr-Scott boiler in mint condition," Jack said enticingly. With few other alternatives open to him, Bob decided he wanted to check it out.

When Jack then mentioned that the boiler was located in British Columbia, Bob was a little taken aback. That was at least 1,500 miles away. Thinking about taking on such a project required some sober second thought. "It looked like a hell of a hard way to get an engine," Bob said. In the end, Bob didn't see any other alternative way to get into tractor collecting. Besides, Bob was a do-it-yourself kind of guy.

The first hurdle Bob had to overcome was figuring out how to get to British Columbia and back within one day. He was a cattle farmer, and the farm chores wouldn't allow him anymore time away from home than that. With some creative scheduling by a travel agent, he arranged a less-than-twenty-four-hour trip.

After getting to Prince George, the town the boiler was in, Bob finally got a chance to get a good look at it. Jack had been right; it was in good shape, and there were quite a few parts to go along with it. The boiler's owner also knew where Bob could get even more parts. So the build-it-yourself steamer project officially started that day, after Bob wrote a check for the boiler. Now all he had to do was get it home.

"I decided to use my 6500 GMC single-axle grain truck to do the job," Bob said. On a long weekend in July, Bob and Brent Allen, a truck-driver friend, set out on the trip west. On their trip through the Rocky Mountains, they pulled into a truck weigh station, just inside the province of British Columbia.

As a truck driver, Brent had been into weigh stations before and told Bob it was a good idea to be nice to the scale men. In fact, Brent even went so far as to buy some fruit from a roadside stand before getting to the inspection point so he could share it with the officer working at the station. After a friendly chat with the officer and telling him their reason for passing through, they continued on their way.

When they finally arrived at their destination, they needed to make a few alterations to the truck in order for the boiler to fit into the truck box. One side of the box had to be removed, but when that was done, one axle shaft was sticking so far out that the box side couldn't be replaced. Bob had to cut a hole in it large enough for the axle to stick through, so they could bolt the side back on. The rest of the parts were then stacked around the boiler. When they were finished loading, Bob tied a red handkerchief to the protruding axle, and they left on the return trip.

Once they were back on the road, the truck was handling poorly, and it became pretty obvious that it was overloaded. On top of that, the load was top heavy and caused the truck to sway as it rounded corners. And with the engine taxed to its limit, the truck struggled to climb the mountain grades.

To make the trip more comfortable, Brent had disconnected the heater hoses from the truck cab before leaving home because it seemed that engine heat managed to find its way into the cab even when the controls were shut off. Still with no air conditioning, the cab was getting hot during the day, but at night in the mountains, Bob and Brent were freezing. Eventually, they found a hotel and pulled in for the night.

The next day, which happened to be Sunday, they were back at the weigh station where they had met the scale officer the previous day. When the officer had a look at the truck and its load, it was clear that more than a few traffic laws had been broken. Bob and Brent were hauling an oversized load without a permit on a Sunday, a day when oversized loads were not even allowed to travel on provincial highways. On top of that, the truck was almost 7,000 pounds overweight.

The scale officer was generous, though. Their friendly encounter the day before had paid off, and they were allowed to continue with only a small fine. Fortunately, that was their only brush with the law, and they made it home safely. The Garr-Scott project was off to a memorable start, to say the least. There was still a long way to go before Bob would be able to fire up a working engine.

And now each time Bob hears Johnny Cash sing about how he stole his Cadillac "One Piece at a Time," he thinks about his Garr-Scott and how it also came one piece at a time.

After unloading the boiler, Bob had it inspected by the local authorities, and it passed with flying colors. After sandblasting it and spraying on a new coat of paint, it was ready for more parts—but first Bob had to find them.

"I still needed a lot of parts: rear wheels, bull gears, and pinions." The list seemed endless. Again, one of Jack Beamish's tips led Bob into Saskatchewan where he found a water tender that a farmer was using to haul water to his livestock.

Then in 1980, a tip from the boiler's previous owner turned up an old steamer in Alberta that was being sold for scrap. "We came home with the differential and counter shaft," Bob said, as well as other essential parts. After Bob made it home with that load, he heard that a rear wheel from the scrapped engine was about five miles away from the wreck, being used as a water trough in a farmyard. Bob turned around and headed back to Alberta to try and convince that farmer to part with it.

The farmer reluctantly agreed to sell it, but getting it freed from its home inside a corral took the pulling power of two large farm tractors. The wheel had concrete poured in it to form a base for the water trough. After the wheel was pulled out into the open, it had to be separated from the concrete base so it could be loaded for transport. Breaking out the concrete "was the hardest day's work I'd done in a long time," Bob said. "Finally, I got the rim loaded on my pickup truck and blew three rear tires hauling it home. At least now I had all the wheels."

Advertising in a variety of magazines paid off, as Bob got a call from Bill Arnett in Haviland, Kansas, who had some valve linkages and other miscellaneous parts to offer. Bill also knew a fellow named George Richey in Norwich, Ohio, who had a mold available for a part Bob needed. George agreed to get the part made and bring it to Bob at a steam show in Ontario.

Bob flew to Ontario to pick up the part, and he found another item he needed at the show. Bob's engine was now taking shape, but he still needed steering parts if the tractor was going to be able to move. Floyd Brudevold in Valley City, North Dakota, offered to remove the steering parts from his Garr-Scott and have molds made so Bob could have new parts fabricated. One by one, Bob either turned up original parts or found a way to have them manufactured. Finally, in 1982, Bob's part-original, part-new Garr-Scott 25-75 fired to life for the first time.

And now each time Bob hears Johnny Cash sing about how he stole his Cadillac "One Piece at a Time," he thinks about his Garr-Scott and how it also came one piece at a time.

CHAPTER EIGHT

Out of Retirement and Back to Work

School's Out

Without question, most farm boys would rather spend time driving the family tractor than doing homework. But other than Sonny Reese, few could honestly say that driving the tractor was their homework.

In 1960, Sonny's dad, Hurschel, ended up buying a plow at a farm auction. One of his father's friends was there and commented that now Hurschel needed a tractor to go with his new plow, and he just happened to have the machine for the job. Of course, it hadn't been running in years.

Seeing an opportunity to gain another piece of machinery at a rock-bottom price, Hurschel decided to leave the auction and go look at his neighbor's tractor. Parked at the neighbor's farm was a 1935 Allis-Chalmers Model WC. The then twenty-five-year-old tractor had sat unused for a long time, and the engine could no longer be turned by the crank. Sonny's father suspected that rainwater had seeped into the engine through the exhaust pipe and caused the pistons to stick. Still for $25, it seemed like a bargain.

After taking the plow home, Hurschel and fourteen-year-old Sonny returned to the neighbor's farm to pick up the old tractor. They hooked a chain to the front, hitched it to the back of Hurschel's 1948 GMC grain truck, and started back down the road to the family farm, with Sonny steering the WC.

The plan was to fix up the WC and use it on the family farm near Downs, Illinois, but by now it was midwinter and there was no heated garage to park the WC in so it could be worked on. And the weather, as Sonny recalled, was "mighty cold."

In a stroke of luck, Sonny needed a project for his freshman agriculture and industrial arts classes at school, and he made a deal with his teachers to bring the WC into town and put it in the workshop at Downs High School. That way the WC could not only get the needed repairs, but it could earn Sonny some high school credits.

This plan did have one drawback. "I got accused of everything from brown-nosing the teachers to get good grades to being a show off," Sonny said. Both were far from the truth. The chance to have the tractor fixed in the

Sonny Reese's 1935 Allis-Chalmers WC sat unused for years in a farmyard near his childhood home. His father paid $25 for it and towed it home with Sonny's help. Then Sonny and his classmates in high school rebuilt the engine, and the tractor went back to working for a living.

school shop was a real bonus for Sonny's family, who were not exactly wealthy.

Once inside the school shop, Sonny, his teachers David Heathers and Donald Sargent, and the rest of the class began tearing down the engine. What they found confirmed Hurschel's suspicions about rainwater getting into the cylinders, and things looked grim for the WC's chances of ever running again. The group continued to dismantle the engine anyway. Once all the pieces were removed, the teachers laid them out along the shop floor and used the parts to teach the students about basic engine design.

During a visit to his grandmother's, one of Sonny's uncles asked about the progress the class had made on the WC. When Sonny explained that the engine may be unsalvageable, his uncle Leonard offered to give Sonny the engine out of a WC he had that no longer ran. Sonny and his father then removed the engine from Leonard's WC and hauled it to the school.

Once both engines were apart, it was clear that the two were not exactly identical; Leonard's WC was a few years newer than Sonny's, and whether or not all the parts would interchange was doubtful, at least in the opinion of the teachers.

Sonny's father, however, decided to make a visit to the school and see what he could do. "So, the next day my dad showed up for ag classes and stepped up and taught the class and teachers about the fine art of parts switchin'—redneck style!" Sonny said. "Then we all had a good time and dug in to see what would fit where. Most everything went in okay, except the block was for a newer tractor, and the old head had one less bolt hole, but that was all. So, dad said it would work, even so."

Many of the students in Sonny's class were just starting to get their driver's licenses, and that meant some had just bought their first cars, most of which were old and needed repairs. As the class members realized they could take the knowledge they gained from repairing the engine in the old WC and use it on their cars; the teasing Sonny had endured for bringing the tractor to school stopped.

And getting the tractor running again became an obsession for the two teachers in charge of the workshop. "They wouldn't give up until we had it running," Sonny said. On the last day of school, the WC was purring like a kitten. Sonny was told to get on it and drive it out the door of the school workshop. One teacher climbed on beside him and leaned against the fender, while the second one stood on the drawbar and held on behind Sonny as the tractor moved out into the school grounds.

"They made me drive around the grounds," he said, adding that two or three physical education classes were outside playing on the ball fields. Sonny wheeled the WC around them as many of his classmates looked on. Then he proceeded past the window of the principal's office, who leaned out to see what was going on. He just smiled and shrugged after Sonny, David, and Donald gave him a big wave.

"We were going all over the place. [The teachers would] say go over by this window or that one. Everyone saw us. We drove past all of my classmates," Sonny said. Now when looking back at that day, when they just happened to drive past every one of the students who had ridiculed him over the old WC, he realizes what his teachers were up to. "I think it was all set up; it had to be. I think by doing that they were saying, 'Hey you guys were always putting him down. Look what can be done if you try,'" he said.

The WC spent many years working on the Reese family farm. "As the tractor herd grew, the WC had an easier life as it had some big brothers to do the heavy stuff; so it mainly became the hay tractor," Sonny said. As times and tractor technology changed, many people in the area were of the notion that their tractors had to be new, fast, and big. Regardless, Sonny's father kept the WC. "Dad was of the type that if it runs, I'll use it," Sonny said.

Eventually, the second engine in the WC wore out, and the tractor was out of a job again. These days, Sonny just doesn't have the heart to sell it. It became his after his father died a few years ago. Sonny and his wife hope to breathe life into it one more time. All the other old tractors from his father's herd have been sold, but not the WC.

Now, the tractor is just outside the kitchen window of Sonny's farmhouse. Maybe catching an occasional glimpse of it brings back memories of that triumphant ride around the school grounds, or maybe of the day Sonny and his father worked together to tow it home, both thinking of the future possibilities for the old hulk. Or maybe Sonny keeps it in view because sometimes it's nice just to have an old friend around.

Two for One

The Allis-Chalmers Model B and C tractors had been sitting beside an old corn crib near Seaman, Ohio, since at least the 1970s. This team of tractors was once the main power for Jake Pense's small farm in southern Ohio. But after Jake died in the mid-1970s, and his wife, Lizzie, followed him a few years later, the tractors' roles had changed. They had become silent memorials to a farmer and his life, rather than functioning machines.

As with most memorials, someone eventually takes notice of them, and the forlorn old tractors were no exception. What follows here is the story of their recovery, as Joe Devore tells it, which starts like this:

Vernon Grimes found the pair of Allis tractors and rescued them from obscurity in the mid-1990s. He made a deal with the remaining members of the Pense family and bought the two neglected machines. Despite his new interest in them, they weren't ready to see any action just yet. Vernon turned the tractors over to Junior Shelton a few days later and let him get to the heart of their mechanical problems. He discovered that the tractors had deteriorated so much they no longer ran.

No one there seemed to recognize the metal gem for what it was, and what's more, it was undamaged and looked salvageable.

Junior Shelton was a retired mechanic who had spent many years in the service garage keeping Dayton's fleet of police cars running at peak efficiency. Vernon apparently figured Junior was just the man to put the two little Allis-Chalmers tractors back into operation. Consequently, Vernon and Junior struck a deal. Junior would repair one for Vernon and keep the other for himself as payment for his mechanical efforts.

Junior had the C operational within a week or two, and Vernon was able to put it back to work. Junior kept the B, which wasn't nearly as easy to get running again. Its engine block was cracked, and the pistons were stuck—really stuck. All in all, the engine was just too far gone to be salvaged, and Junior thought it would never drink gasoline again.

For a while, it seemed the B wouldn't be anything more than a parts donor, until Junior made a fortunate find at a local auction sale. An Allis-Chalmers engine block from another B had been thrown in with a pile of scrap metal at the sale. No one there seemed to recognize the metal gem for what it was, and what's more, it was undamaged and looked salvageable. After giving it a close inspection and confirming the block was still useable, Junior outbid those who were only willing to pay scrap-steel value for the lot. He took the block home to give Jake Pense's old B a chance for a new life. Once the block was installed, the tractor was running again, just like it had been those many years ago.

Then in 1996, Joe Devore was in the market for a small cultivating tractor, and he heard Junior had one for sale, so he went to have a look. Junior now wanted to sell the B, and it was perfect for Joe's needs. The two men made a deal, and the B went home with Joe and was put into action in his tobacco field.

Now the B is a trusty farm worker once more—a pretty remarkable comeback for a tractor that was nearly written off as a parts donor.

Overseas Transplants

Jeff Jones' ranch near the town of 100-Mile House in the interior region of British Columbia is a long way from his native England. Jeff immigrated to Canada thirty-five years ago and settled down in Vancouver. But after years of the hustle and bustle of city life, Jeff was ready to return to a slower pace.

Having been born and raised on a farm, he couldn't resist the lure of a quiet, rural existence. So in 1995, after some searching for just the right place, Jeff and his wife pulled up stakes and moved to their new home, far away from the bright lights of the big city.

Jeff's new ranch came complete with two old tractors— a 1951 John Deere styled Model AR and a 1948 Farmall Cub—and a line of haying equipment. But doing all the work needed to put up hay for his animals and run the ranch with the somewhat temperamental AR proved to be a bit of a chore for Jeff. The AR wasn't equipped with a live power take-off, and using it to bale hay was difficult in conditions where the swath size varied.

Selecting a higher gear for lighter swaths would overload the baler when the swath became heavy. To avoid

Hiding in an abandoned farmyard, this 135 Massey had seen better days. The electrical system was a mess. And to top it off, it had an uncommon Lucas electrical system used only on British models, which meant this tractor should have been on the other side of the Atlantic.

breaking shear pins, Jeff had to veer out of the swath and stop to change gears. The thought of using a more modern tractor for haying was beginning to have a real appeal after a few seasons of struggling with the AR.

In 2004, an ad in a local paper for a 1965 Massey-Ferguson 135 caught Jeff's eye. When he called the seller and asked about its condition, the seller said, "The tractor was running when it was parked six or seven years ago." "Yeah, right," Jeff thought. Still maybe there was a chance to get a newer tractor at an economical price, as long as it didn't need too much work.

As the conversation continued, the seller said something strange: "I'm selling it for a friend." Immediately, alarm bells sounded in Jeff's mind. Yet despite his doubts, he decided to go ahead and have a look at the tractor anyway.

Of course, finding the little Massey proved to be no easy task. The seller gave Jeff a detailed set of directions, which led him down an unfamiliar road well off the beaten path. After driving a few miles along the dirt road, Jeff turned off and crossed a couple of open fields, went through an abandoned farmyard, and traveled still farther across country. Finally, Jeff found himself in a second abandoned homestead.

This farmyard looked to be a turn-of-the-century creation. The house, barn, and outbuildings were built from squared-off timbers, no doubt hand cut from the surrounding stands of trees. Most of the buildings had collapsed onto themselves, and Jeff found himself watching squirrels scurry out of the old house. Apparently, he had disturbed the long-standing peace of the old yard with his arrival.

Parked in the decaying yard, backed up to an old fence, was the tractor he came to see. The 135 looked a little neglected, to say the least. It was covered with grass seeds from years of haying duties, and the tall grass of the abandoned farmyard was now growing around it. The tractor wasn't alone in the old yard. The site was a veritable graveyard of long-forgotten farm machinery, with an old disker, a baler, and a host of other implements now hiding in the tall grass and bushes.

Turning his interest back to the 135, Jeff noticed its first defect: Its ignition switch was dangling from wires instead of being firmly attached in its place. Looking at the mass of wires behind the dash of the tractor, Jeff realized that a major short circuit had inflicted a lot of damage, welding the frayed wires together in places and making a mess out of a once-functioning system. Yet other than this problem, the 135 looked promising, and Jeff decided to buy it.

Today, Jeff Jones' 135 is a far cry from what it was when he found it abandoned deep in the heart of a neighbor's ranch land. Even though Jeff and the little tractor are both British at heart, neither is likely to leave their British Columbia ranch anytime soon.

After recontacting the seller, Jeff found out who the tractor's owner was and to his astonishment that owner lived only about one mile from where the 135 had been left to sit out several seasons. The trip to the owner's home, however, was relatively short and simple, compared to where the little Massey sat—the off-the-beaten-path farmyard Jeff had made a complicated trek to earlier. Jeff also realized why the owner was having someone else sell the tractor for him—he was nearly deaf, so having a phone conversation about the 135 would have been almost impossible. Regardless, Jeff managed to make himself heard and struck a deal for the tractor. He would pay $2,200 for it, as long as the engine wasn't stuck.

After getting a tow rope, a spare battery, and his neighbor, Henry, to help pull the tractor home, Jeff returned to the old farmyard. He hoped to be able to tow the tractor the five miles or so back to his ranch. He only brought the battery along to see if the starter would turn the engine over, so he could ensure the pistons weren't seized. Whether or not the mangled wiring would allow the starter to work was another question.

After the two men attached the tractor's old cables to the battery and jumped the starter terminals with a screwdriver, the engine easily spun over. Jeff pushed in the fuel cut-off button, and the tractor immediately fired and ran, startling both Jeff and Henry. Their surprise could certainly be understood, considering the diesel fuel in the tank had been in there since the tractor was parked in that spot seven years before.

After recovering from the shock of seeing the diesel engine idle steadily, they swapped the tow rope for a slow-moving-vehicle sign, and Jeff climbed onto the 135 and drove it home without a glitch.

While negotiating the purchase, Jeff found out the 135 was used by the former owner to do general farm chores on his ranch. He also realized that it had to have a more unusual past—it was a British edition of a 135, not a typical North American one.

Because it was a British model, the 135's electrical system was considerably different than the North American model's. Jeff's 135 had Lucas electrics rather than a Delco system. It was a stroke of bad luck, considering the shape the electricals were in. Yet amazingly, the tractor's previous owner told Jeff the system had been that way for years, and he hadn't bothered to fix it.

Finding all the right parts for the British system made Jeff do a bit more legwork. Yet because Jeff had so many family members still living in England and because he tracked down a diagram of the tractor's electrical wiring, the job didn't prove to be too difficult. No doubt, the unfamiliar electrical system and the difficulty in sourcing parts contributed to the 135 being literally put out to pasture before Jeff found it.

With the electricals now in working order, the little Massey has assumed its position as the flagship of the tractor fleet on Jeff Jones' ranch, making baling hay a much more civilized operation.

An Extra Dexta

For years, Ken Wingert would drive by a 1958 Fordson Dexta that was just sitting unused in a yard, and each time he would pass, it would bother him.

Ken, a mechanic, had spent most of his career working for Ford tractor dealers in Regina, Saskatchewan, so he had a special fondness for the little British-built Dexta tractors. "They're very good tractors," Ken said. Dextas were the smallest of the tractor line offered by Fordson at the time, powered by a three-cylinder, 144-cubic-inch P3 Perkins that put out 32 horses.

The one particular Dexta that caught Ken's attention had been abandoned to a grassy corner of a farmyard only one and a half miles down the road from his farm—so close, yet so far. On top of that, Ken had worked on that very tractor when his former neighbor, the tractor's original owner, brought it into the dealership where Ken worked.

He had known Reinhold Deoge, the original owner, but eventually Reinhold retired from farming. When he sold his farm, Reinhold made a package deal with the buyer. The new owner purchased everything, including the machinery.

Even though Fordson Dextas are uncommon in North America these days, the owner of this one apparently had no love for the little tractor. He abandoned it in a distant corner of his farmyard. The tractor was included in the purchase of some farmland he acquired several years ago.

Even though the little Dexta had been the farm's main power unit when Reinhold ran things, the new owner had a different idea. He parked the tractor in an out-of-the-way spot and simply ignored it. The Dexta had become a surplus item on the farm where at one time it was the only working tractor. Apparently, in the new owner's eyes, it wasn't one of the more prized acquisitions that came with the land.

With a career spent working on tractors just like the Fordson, Ken couldn't bear to see the little machine wasting away. Clearly, it needed to be rescued.

"One day, I just went in and asked [the new owner] if he'd sell it," Ken said. "I think he was happy I took it off his hands. I think it was just too small for him to farm with."

As farms have generally increased in size over the last few decades, many tractors like the small Dexta have found themselves being replaced by higher-horsepower models. This Dexta seemed to have been no exception.

Once Ken ushered the Dexta into his farm workshop, he set to work taking it apart to fully take stock of its condition. Although the tractor had clocked a lot of hours, "there really wasn't anything wrong with it," Ken said. Even the sheet metal was well preserved, with no serious rust. Nevertheless, he decided to give it an overhaul anyway. After Ken replaced the pistons and rods and checking out the hydraulic system and driveline, the Dexta was ready for new paint.

Because the tractor needed little work, Ken was pleased with the outcome of his efforts. "Everything is original," he said. He was so pleased, in fact, that he made another trip down the road to visit the neighbor who sold him the tractor. "I went back and asked if he wanted to sell the implements," he said.

Because Reinhold had originally used the tractor for field work, he had acquired several three-point-hitch implements to pull behind it. They were still hiding in the grass in Reinhold's old farmyard. The new owner hadn't paid much attention to them either, so it wasn't too hard to convince him to part with them. That second trip to the neighbor netted Ken a good haul. He came home with a Ferguson two-furrow plow, a Massey-Harris double disk, and a Ford 7-foot cultivator.

After its temporary hiatus from farm work, Ken put the Dexta back into service. It hasn't exactly replaced his main farm tractor, but the little Fordson now does double duty cutting grass and cultivating small patches of land around Ken's farmyard. Ken's Dexta is equipped with both the optional live-PTO and live-hydraulic systems, making it every bit as good as a modern equivalent—except for the absence of power steering. After a good scrubbing, he takes it to town, so to speak: He shows it in local antique tractor events.

Produced from 1957 to 1964, around 150,000 little blue workhorses came out of Ford's plant in England. Starting in 1962, some later-model Dextas were imported to the United States and badged as Model 2000s, possibly a more familiar sight to many North American farmers.

Even with about 10,400 hours on the clock, Ken's workhorse still gets lots of attention at tractor shows, usually because it's the only Dexta there.

Rusting under a
Willow Tree

Ralph Roggenbuck can remember working in the same field as a little 1939 Ford 9N tractor as a kid. The Ford was owned by Art, a farmer who lived only a mile down the road from the farm Ralph grew up on, near Carpio, North Dakota, and as was common a few decades ago, many farmers shared their equipment during harvest.

Yet while Ralph was still a youngster, the farmer who owned the Ford passed away, and none of his family wanted to remain on the farm. Consequently, the little tractor and much of the farm's equipment were abandoned, left to sit unused. The Ford was parked under a willow tree.

Because Art's farm was so close to the Roggenbuck farm, Ralph walked past the willow tree and the Ford many times. He saw the tractor deteriorating there for three or four years.

"My dad had been talking to the banker [handling Art's estate], and the subject of Art's equipment came up," Ralph said. "Pretty soon the banker asked Dad if he was

---

Ralph says his first thought on seeing the little tractor arrive in the family farmyard was that his father had wasted $75. By now, the tractor looked like a hopeless case.

---

interested in the tractor. So they ended up with a deal."

Ralph's father paid the banker $75 for the little Ford, and one afternoon late in the summer, Ralph's father and older brother went to get the tractor from under the willow tree. After pumping up one tire, they hooked the tractor to the rear of a pickup truck and pulled it home. "They used an old bootlegger's trick," Ralph said. They ran a length of chain through a piece of pipe to keep the two machines a constant distance apart while the tractor was being towed.

Ralph says his first thought on seeing the little tractor arrive in the family farmyard was that his father had wasted $75. By now, the tractor looked like a hopeless case. It even had a bit of a lean to it. Apparently, though, Ralph's father had seen some potential in it.

Within about a week of getting the tractor home, it was rolled into the farm's workshop, and the repair work began. There were more than a few problems to sort out. First on the list was to get the tires properly inflated and replace one that was beyond repair. That got rid of the lean. Although there were some serious cracks in the 11.00x28 rear Co-op-brand tires, they ended up lasting for several years after the tractor was eventually put back to work on the Roggenbuck farm.

The fuel tank also no longer held fuel and required some soldering to patch a couple of leaks. One of the rear wheel rims was leaking as the result of extensive corrosion and required replacing.

There were still remnants of a taillight on the rear of one of the fenders, which had been broken off by a buck rake that Art had used on the three-point hitch. Apparently, the rake's design allowed it to be lifted so high it hit the light. The headlights that used to be mounted on the front of the tractor were missing, too. All of these flaws didn't add to the tractor's visual appeal.

And the tractor had an odd, additional feature. It had an extra drawbar mounted on the front. No one was quite sure what Art had used that for.

After Ralph's father replaced some ignition parts and refilled the repaired fuel tank, the tractor started and ran. With all of the mechanical problems taken care of, Ralph's father broke out his paint brush and gave the tractor a new coat of gray paint to improve its appearance. The brushed-on job wouldn't win any awards, but it did freshen up the look of the old 9N.

Ralph eventually put in more than a few hours in the driver's seat of the Ford and remembers a few of its idiosyncrasies. "The clutch and left brake were both on the left side. I used to rip the edge of my pants on the brake while hitting the clutch," he said. "And it was the fastest of those little Fords I had ever been on. It would nearly keep up with a Farmall M in road gear—of course, young kids ran them wide open!"

The Ford's three-point hitch proved a useful addition to the farm's workforce; it was something none of the other tractors on the Roggenbuck farm had. Ralph says he can recall seeing the tractor used for a variety of chores, from hauling feed to the barn and wood for the stove in the farmhouse to carrying young calves out of the pasture. Ralph remembers that the tractor was great for fence repairs, too. It could get into spots where Ralph's father was reluctant to drive the family pickup truck.

Soon, the family put the Ford to work mowing and raking hay, even baling straw and cultivating corn fields, all tasks that demanded a little more serious output from the tractor's four-cylinder engine.

The $75 investment, along with a few days' repair work, had given the family a reliable workhorse that stayed on the farm until Ralph's father died many years later. Some time after that, the tractor was sold. "I have no real idea where it went," Ralph said.

One thing seems certain: The little 9N Ford is one of those tractors that made a lasting impression on a young boy. Even though decades have passed since that time, Ralph still has fond memories of the little tractor that was rescued from where it was left to rust under a willow tree.

CHAPTER NINE

Some Personal Favorites

As a boy growing up on a prairie farm in the 1970s, the one thing that fascinated me more than anything else was tractors, which wouldn't have surprised anyone who knew me at the time.

The walls in my bedroom were plastered with pictures of tractors cut from the advertisements in various farming magazines. Looking back on it, that seems like a pretty normal thing to do. But in comparison, most of my friends had the infamous Farrah Fawcett poster on their walls, so I guess my passion for tractors was a little more intense than that of my peers.

In my never-ending quest to find new tractor photographs to add to the decor in my bedroom, I was

A Cockshutt 30, equipped with a loader, is one of several machines that sit parked in this old farmyard. The farm and its equipment were abandoned years ago, so the tractors and implements were simply left where they were last parked.

pleased to see that a new magazine was being delivered to our postal box. It was a short-lived one, with a lot of farm machinery advertising in it. The best thing about it was that each ad had a number, and in the center of the magazine was a mail-in card with corresponding numbers. If you wanted more information about the products in any advertisement, you just circled the appropriate number and sent the card in to the magazine, postage free!

That was just too good to be true. I needed more tractor pictures for my walls, and all those free manufacturers' brochures were bound to have some great shots. So I circled the number of anything even remotely interesting and dropped the cards in the mail when I happened to be in town.

Before long, I amassed an impressive collection of brochures and was getting more great pictures. My parents weren't too sure about the whole thing, but the process went along smoothly for a couple of months. Then, in one issue there was an ad for Steiger tractors, promoting one of their newest models: the Bearcat. I just had to have a picture of that, so away went the information card. Not too long after, I received a couple of corporate brochures and a polite letter telling me not to hesitate to contact my local dealer for a test drive.

I wasn't going to press my luck and try that. I was only about fourteen years old! No dealer would seriously consider me a potential buyer. But I'd buy one eventually, I thought, for the massive farm I would someday own. So I convinced myself that the company's expense of sending me some brochures would pay off in the long run.

Then the whole free-pictures thing collapsed on me. After the school bus dropped me off at home one day, my father was waiting for me. The look on his face let me know, without a doubt, that I was in trouble. It seems the Steiger company had passed my name on to the local Steiger dealer as a potential customer, and not knowing who I was, the dealer made a trip out to the farm one afternoon to see if he could sell me a Bearcat. Of course, I was in school.

When the salesman asked my father if I was interested in buying a new tractor, my whole free-pictures scam was exposed. Not surprisingly, I was never allowed to mail in another information-reply card until I grew up and left home. To this day whenever I see one of those mail-in cards, I get shivers up my spine.

That was a long time ago, and I never did get a Bearcat. But that love of tractors stayed with me. Nowadays, if I can't own all the ones I want, I can at least write about them. And over the years, a few memorable tractor-finding stories have come my way. Some of them mine, some passed on from others. Here are some of my favorites.

The Auction Lottery

This is one is mine, and it's probably the first and most memorable tractor story I can think of.

Back in the early 1970s, I remember my grandfather, father, brother, and me heading off on a summer afternoon to a large auction sale held in a town about forty-five minutes away from our farm. I was about twelve years old and my brother was ten. I'd been to a couple of farm-dispersal sales, but this one was gigantic by comparison. It was a consignment sale held at a machinery dealership.

Even though I was only twelve, I was already smitten with all things mechanical. Having a chance to be among this collection of unfamiliar machines, to walk around them and sit in the driver's seats and imagine driving around a field on the family farm in them, was more than memorable.

Oddly enough, I can remember seeing a pair of Claas Yellow Fellow self-propelled combines there. At the time, they looked absolutely enormous. They seemed as large then as that company's Lexion line of monster machines seem to me today. Now, when I see one of these old yellow machines sitting in the bush behind some farmyard, I

Looking like it's still waiting to be refueled, this Massey-Harris 30 appears to have been forgotten. Only its weathered look and the growth of plants around it suggest the passage of so much time since it was last running.

can't help but wonder why I thought they were so big; in comparison to today's machines, they're absolutely tiny.

But I also remember this sale for another big reason: The auction company decided to hold a raffle in an attempt to draw in the crowds. The company was going to give away a Ford 9N tractor. Everyone who attended could buy a ticket and have a chance to win it. My grandfather decided to buy four tickets. When he came back from buying them, he handed each of us one.

This McCormick Super W-6 ended up hiding behind rows of hay and straw bales in my cousin's farmyard after its engine seized. Eventually, I found out it was the same tractor I had spent many hours on while growing up. As an old family member, it deserved a new lease on life.

At the end of the afternoon, when all the machines had sold, the remaining crowd stood around the auctioneer's stand and listened intently as he reached into a bucket and pulled out a ticket stub. The holder of the winning ticket would take home the little Ford.

As he slowly called out the numbers, I was staring intently at my ticket. One by one the numbers matched; my heart rate increased exponentially with each match. Then, incredibly, there was only one more number to go and the 9N would be mine! I was pretty excited, to say the least. But when the last number was read out, I was one digit off.

Before I could get too frustrated at being so close yet so far, my brother raised his hand and yelled, "I have it!"

Sure enough, he had the winning ticket. However, there was one more hurdle to overcome before he could claim the tractor. Local law required the winner of a raffle to answer a "skill testing" question—whatever gave rise to such a requirement, I'll never know. My brother bravely moved up to the podium and stood next to the auctioneer to have his skill tested. This could be trouble, I thought. Then it came, the question that everything hinged on. I crossed my fingers. "Does water run uphill or down?" the auctioneer asked. Even my brother knew that one!

A few days later, a truck pulled into our farmyard, and the little gray Ford rolled off to join my father's McCormick Super W-6 and create a farm fleet of two tractors. Despite missing the winning number by one, I had the chance to spend more than a few hours in the driver's seat of the Ford, helping with field work.

Oddly enough, despite being the only ten-year-old boy in the area to be able to say he owned his own set of wheels, my brother never did get his driver's license. Now he lives in the center of Canada's largest city and has no need for one.

Incoming Minneapolis

This story was told to me by Ken Johnston, another tractor enthusiast.

Ken took a trip to a tractor show in Crosby, North Dakota, in the mid-1980s and had a chance encounter with an elderly gentleman who was standing beside a very early example of one of Minneapolis-Moline's finest early gas tractors. He seemed to be trying to figure out how to best photograph the old tractor. For some reason, the man attracted Ken's attention.

Noticing the camera, Ken asked the old gentleman if he would like to have his picture taken with the machine. The fellow eagerly accepted the offer. Curious, Ken asked why he was so interested in the Minneapolis.

The response started off routinely enough. He had been raised on a farm, and his father had a Minneapolis, just like the one on display. After several years, it was worn out and, therefore, parked in a scrub of trees near the farmyard to rest in peace. After the tractor spent a few neglected years there, the scrap-metal market heated up in the late 1930s due to an increased demand for steel from Japan. The fellow's father saw an opportunity to cash the old Minneapolis in for a few dollars, and he sold it to a scrap-iron dealer who was making the rounds. Later on, it became widely known where most of the scrap metal was going and why: Japan needed it for its prewar buildup in armaments. The thought of the old tractor contributing to a then-enemy's fortunes stuck in the craw of the man and his family.

As he continued to relate the story about the old Minneapolis to Ken, the man said he eventually enlisted in the U.S. Army and saw active service in the South Pacific. At that point, he paused for a moment and looked squarely at Ken. Then, he said every time he sheltered himself from another salvo of enemy bombardments, he could only think of one thing: "Here comes that damn Minneapolis again!"

After repairing a couple of flat tires, Davey and I towed the Super W-6 down the road and into my workshop. Now the restoration process begins, and the tractor is home once again after being away nearly three decades.

Ready and Waiting

Early last autumn, I was just settling down for a Sunday afternoon in front of the television to watch the home team play a football game when my neighbor called. Was I busy, he asked, because he needed a favor. Would I help him move his son's tractor and baler a few miles west to a rented field where it would be put to work on Monday baling straw? For as much as I knew this was going to be a good game, and it was my team, I was certainly obligated to go and help him. So I did.

After we delivered the tractor and baler to the proper location, we jumped into his pickup truck and headed back toward the main road, which led home. As we got to the corner, my neighbor stopped the truck before making the turn. "There's something I have to show you," he said. "You're not in a hurry, are you?"

So much for catching the second half of the game. "No," I said half-heartedly. So instead of turning and heading back east, we went farther west.

A few miles up the road, we turned off onto a dirt trail, which led a mile or more along the edge of a grain field. "I know you like old tractors, so I thought I should show you this," he said. As the dirt road wound around a grove of trees, there it was: an absolutely unique scene. It's one that vintage-tractor hunters sometimes dream about but rarely find: an old, abandoned farmyard, complete with tractors, that looked almost as it did forty or more years ago. Almost everything, including the machinery, had been left as it was, and due to the secluded and sometimes inaccessible location, few people ever ventured into the yard or even knew it existed.

My neighbor's son had recently rented this land, and the yard was just as he found it that spring. A Massey-Harris Model 30 was parked beside an overhead fuel tank, as if waiting for refueling after a day in the field. A Cockshutt 30, with an attached front-end loader, was parked in line with a few old implements and a John Deere 65 pull-type combine. The farmhouse and barn were still firmly standing, too, along with a few old sheds. It was as though the farmer had finished work for the day and gone inside for a Sleeping Beauty–like sleep that lasted decades, while his tractors sat in the overgrown grass just waiting for him to come back out.

In reality, the farmer had simply moved off the farm and later died. He left the farm and everything on it to his daughter, who lived hundreds of miles away and apparently had no intention of ever returning. The farmland had been rented out to various people for years, and the rusting old equipment had just been ignored. By the time the farmer stopped working the land himself, the equipment was too old and too small to be of any real interest to anyone, so it just sat where it was left.

When I finally made it home, I had to tell my wife about the adventure I just had. She just looked at me a little curiously and asked, "Don't you want to know the score in the game?"

The Tractor in the Haystack

I'd often seen the old McCormick Super W-6 that had been sitting, unused, in my cousin Davey's farmyard during the past few years, but I hadn't given it too much thought. I either already had a project in the workshop or had a long list of other things to do. To even consider adding something else to that list always seemed like a pretty low priority. Aside from that, my cousin hadn't mentioned wanting to sell it.

It had been parked in his barnyard for years, and one day I happened to notice it was gone. When I asked about

Once the head was removed from the engine, I got a look at the cylinders. The number three exhaust valve was stuck open, and that cylinder had filled with water. The others were nearly full of flaked rust and dirt. Getting the engine running again will definitely take some effort.

it, Davey said he just wanted to get it out of the way, so he pulled it around to the side of the yard where he stacked his hay bales.

It was now hidden from passers-by, but when spring arrived and most of the bales had been used up, you could just barely see it. The tractor was definitely starting to look a little worse for having been exposed to the elements during all those years. And like any other tractor enthusiast, the thought of what it could look like if I could get my hands

240

on it crossed my mind more than a few times.

Finally, I happened to be visiting, and the topic of conversation got around to the old McCormick. "It was Johnny's tractor," Davey said. Johnny was his brother, a veteran who had died many years ago.

Then this question arose: When did he get it? Everyone began trying to think back to when Johnny had bought the tractor new. The early 1950s was everyone's best guess. Then someone suggested looking at the owner's manual to see if the year of the tractor's manufacture was written in it. Amazingly, the original manual was in a drawer just out of arm's reach from where we were all sitting talking about the McCormick.

When Davey handed me the manual, I was struck by some handwriting on the front of it. It was my father's. "Yeah, it was your dad's tractor, too," he said. That meant this was the tractor I had spent many hours on when I was growing up.

I can still remember first seeing the used Super W-6 sitting on a J. I. Case dealer's lot in 1972. The school bus would pass by that dealership every morning as I rode in to school. There were three W-Series IH tractors parked side by side on the lot at that time. All three looked nearly new, and their bright red paint stood out among a sea of Desert Sand–colored Case tractors that also occupied the lot.

One day that year, my father bought the Super W-6, and it became the main tractor on the farm until a 3020 John Deere took over. No one could remember exactly how the W-6 ended up on the lot after Johnny died, but another cousin remembered driving him to the nearby IH dealership in 1953 to pick up the tractor, which, according to the serial number, was built in 1952.

All of these family ties to the tractor meant that I just had to make an offer on it. After the deal was made, Davey capped it off by saying, "If you get it running again, I'll give you your money back." I'm not too set on ever taking him up on that promise; the price I paid was a nominal one, at best. However, the tractor will definitely run again!

When I first inspected it, I found that the engine was stuck because of the amount of rainwater that had seeped into the manifold. The tractor also had a couple of flat tires that had to be repaired before it could be towed down the road and into my workshop. Well, I guess there was room in there for one more project after all.

As I write this, the Super W-6's engine is soaking in penetrating fluid. I have no doubt the crankshaft will soon be turning, and it will fire to life again before too long.

With its heritage, the McCormick is a tractor well worth a restoration effort. After all, it's a piece of family history.

There Are Still Treasures Out There

It's a common sight: a semi-trailer truck traveling down a highway with a cargo of old tractors heading for parts unknown. Trucks like that have been hauling away old machines for a couple of decades now, at pretty regular intervals.

The days of finding an old Deere hiding in the trees behind every homestead, abandoned or otherwise, are over. Vintage tractors of all brands are being sought out and hauled away, spawning an entire industry of buying and selling them. Old tractors now sail across the oceans in both directions, some leaving for foreign shores and others arriving to take their places.

Of course, like any collectible commodity, the strength of the vintage-tractor market fluctuates with the times. However, overall, the iron and steel recyclers have been largely robbed of this traditional source of raw material. In

Hiding in plain sight, these five tractors have been sitting beside the Trans-Canada Highway at Virden, Manitoba, for decades. It's hard to believe no one has bought them yet and hauled them home and restored them. There are some great old models in this group.

the past, more than a few old tractors were melted down at steel mills around the world to provide the basic metals for new cars and skyscrapers, among other things. And seeing that trend slow to a trickle certainly lifts the spirits of anyone with an appreciation for mechanized history.

With any luck, the hobby will continue to strengthen, and those venerable old tractors will be well cared for long after their expected lifespan as a working machine has elapsed, even if the hardest work they do is march proudly in a parade.

And there's nothing wrong with keeping these old tractors around for a life of relative leisure; everyone's entitled to a retirement. Of course, these pieces of old iron offer much more than just a place to mount a flower box or where the outdoor Christmas lights are strung in the front yard.

Their worth seems to be more than the sum of their parts. Old tractors are a part of our history, and like any memento of the past, they evoke thoughts of times, family, and friends gone by. Seeing an old tractor crushed and consumed by a blast furnace makes the past feel even more distant.

Thankfully, there is no reason to believe that old tractors are extinct just yet. Far from it. Aside from the many that are now in the capable hands of enthusiasts and collectors all around the world, there are still more than a few forgotten ones hiding out there, just waiting for salvation.

So let me paraphrase—and slightly modify—the words of that well-known author and shipwreck hunter

One of a few old machines occupying an abandoned farmyard near Regina, Saskatchewan, this Cockshutt 30 isn't quite complete, but it's still worth salvaging. At the very least, it would make a great parts donor.

This forgotten Massey is missing a battery, but that's about all. Of course, it's hard to say what kind of mechanical condition the tractor is in. Once restored, this machine is large enough to take on some serious work to repay the effort.

Clive Cussler: Get up off the couch and go into the woods, farm fields, and pastures and hunt for those old tractors. (Clive would have mentioned lakes and oceans and said shipwrecks instead of tractors, but you get the idea.) Bring them home and spend some time making them shine again. Exploit the opportunities those old tractors offer.

What better activity could there be for a father to share with a son than getting a little greasy while making something old and derelict look and run like new again? Working together toward that kind of achievement creates exactly the right environment to help mold young minds. It's a chance to teach the value of creating rather than destroying, while building self-confidence and character.

Parked in the shade of a tree behind a farmyard, this McCormick looks like a very easy project. It's complete, and the tin work is straight. Even the tires are pretty good!

If your favorite color of iron is yellow, there are still a few vintage Minneapolis-Molines out there, like this one north of Winnipeg, Manitoba. It's just a matter of keeping an eye out for gems like this one when traveling along a rural highway. That's how my friend Austin found it.

Restoring a Deere, like this one, has one big advantage over other brands: Thousands of parts for pre-1960 tractors are still available at your local dealer. All you have to do is walk in and order them.

And allowing someone to discover the rewards of freeing a rusted bolt is a lesson that can last a lifetime.

When you really stop and think about it, the tractor is the ultimate machine for creating. That's just what it was designed to do: to provide the power needed to make lush crops grow from black dirt, to turn an empty field into a productive one, to help create something from nothing. Even in their rusted, broken-down form, they can inspire that sentiment and foster a special motivation in those who choose to work on them.

So do yourself a favor: Put an old tractor in your workshop. They're still out there waiting for you to find and save them. To prove it, my friend, Austin Brown, and I took our cameras and went looking, and pictured in this epilogue are just a few examples of what we found in a short amount of time.

Good hunting and good luck.

How to Find Hidden Old Iron

Now that you're primed and ready to go tractor hunting, just how do you do it? Well, there are the want ads, of course. But if you really want to rescue your machine from anonymity behind a haystack, here are some tips that just might help you find that previously hidden gem.

1. Tell your friends. Simply letting people know you're interested in old iron can pay some unexpected dividends. It's truly amazing how many people will tell you they know of something you might be interested in. Even if they don't, word gets around, and you may get a call out of the blue from someone wanting to get rid of an old tractor that's been cluttering up their yard for way too long.

A tractor came my way for that very reason. Unexpectedly, my neighbor came over one day to give us some ears of corn he picked from his garden. As he was about to leave he said, "By the way, do you want that old 55 Massey? I know you like rebuilding tractors."

The tractor had been sitting between some old buildings in his farmyard for nearly as long as I can remember. When I said sure, his reply was, "Well if you can get it running, you can have it." After a carburetor overhaul, a portable tank full of air to re-inflate the tires, some minor tinkering, and a few gallons of antifreeze to fill the radiator, I drove the tractor home on a brisk fall afternoon.

2. Take a drive. Ever have a Sunday afternoon when you really don't know what to do with yourself? Even with our busy modern schedules, it happens now and again. When it does, hop in your pickup truck—or SUV, as the case may be—and go for a drive. But not down the usual paths you travel. Pick one of those roads you always meant to go down, just to see what's there, and drive slowly.

If traffic is light, or more likely nonexistent on many rural roads, you can take your time and survey the scenery. Pay attention to the edges of long-established farmyards. There are often discarded machines and vehicles sitting there; some are salvageable, some not.

3. Attend farm auction sales. I enjoy spending a day at a farm dispersal auction. These are sales held by retiring farmers or those just quitting the business. These are as much a social event as an opportunity to purchase great stuff. Grab a hot dog and a coffee and wander around. Often, old pieces of machinery or some really rare parts end up among the items to sell, without being advertised. And that usually means a bargain can be had, if you know what

you're looking at. The same items at a special collector's sale will often cost much more money.

And it's not uncommon to see an old tractor or truck in the bushes nearby that isn't on the sale listing. The owner may be willing to sell it to you anyway. People may have thought it wasn't worth the effort required to pull it out of the grass, expecting no one would want it.

4. Join a club. There are literally dozens of small groups of vintage machinery enthusiasts all around North America. They hold rallies and show days, usually on a regular basis. If you're not into joining clubs, at least go to a few shows. They are terrific places to network with other enthusiasts. Not all of them want to keep adding to their collections, and some may be downsizing and willing to sell you something you're really interested in.

On occasion, collectors end up with a machine they didn't really want. For example, something may have come to them grouped with another tractor they were after, otherwise they wouldn't have bothered with it. On one occasion, I went out to a collector's acreage just to look at his extensive tractor collection. As I was about to leave, he pointed to a single machine parked a short distance away. "You don't want to buy that, do you?" he asked.

For $100 I took home a new project, which was exactly what I'd been hoping to find. The collector wasn't interested in the brand and just wanted to be rid of it.

Even if no one is in a selling mood, these clubs are repositories of great technical knowledge. Many of the members are skilled mechanics and can give you valuable tips on your project, or even lend a hand. And it seems that at least one of the club members is always a recognized authority on one particular brand or another. I can't remember how many times I've heard something like this: "Oh you have a Case/Massey/John Deere, you should talk to . . ."

5. Take an airplane ride. Admittedly, we don't all have a friend who just happens to be a pilot with his own plane. Yet if you do, or you have your own pilot's license, it's amazing what a change of perspective can reveal in the countryside. And remember, most small cities have a flying school, where you can hire an instructor to take you up for a ride on an hourly basis.

If you happen to be near to such a facility, you could fly over the surrounding countryside scanning for hidden Deeres. Take a map with you and mark the location of anything of interest that catches your eye, then go back and knock on the door. What's the worst that can happen? If the farm dog doesn't bite you when you step out of your car, ask the owner if he would sell the old tractor you just happened to notice while you were flying over. If he says no, move on.

Of course, there may be a quicker way: Cash in on someone else's flights. If there's a crop dusting business in the area, stop in and ask the pilot if he's seen anything of interest while spraying. These guys are buzzing around at tree-top level over the same countryside year after year.

In the end, you're only limited by your imagination. Take advantage of your opportunities. Maybe your job has you reading electrical meters in farmyards or puts you in contact with people who are likely to help you with your quest. Striking up a friendly conversation will not only give you a chance to subtly inquire about old tractors, but it also will make you seem like a pleasant guy working for a friendly company.

I once had a job that required I travel around the Gulf Islands off Canada's west coast in a small boat. Another co-worker, who was also interested in restoring old vehicles, and I would always travel together and scour the properties along the shore for old vehicles that looked like they no longer had the love of their owner. When we found one, it only took a minute to stop in and inquire. We found quite a few interesting machines that way. Our boss knew of our interests and actually assigned us to this type of work quite frequently. No one else wanted to do it anyway. So we took care of a job he couldn't get anyone to do, and we had a chance to mix business with pleasure. In fact, we had a blast!

The point here is take advantage of the opportunities that present themselves. Even if you go down a hundred dead ends for every successful one, there's excitement in the hunt. And you're doing something you like. Really, isn't that what life is all about?

INDEX